FOR MEN ONLY

not just provider but participant

by
Harry Salem II

For men, fathers, husbands, sons,
who want a real relationship with their loved ones,
and ultimately God

Unless otherwise indicated, all Scripture quotations are taken from the *King James Version* of the Bible.

For Men Only — not just provider, but participant
ISBN 1-890370-01-0
Copyright © 1997
Salem Family Ministries
P.O. Box 701287
Tulsa, Oklahoma 74170

TABLE OF CONTENTS

Chapter One 7
The Crisis That Changed My Life

Chapter Two 18
God Has Provided You With A Supernatural Covering

Chapter Three 26
Provider Or Participant...The Tough Decision For Men Today

Chapter Four 31
Do You Want To Be A Father or a Dad?

Chapter Five..41
How To Become A Good Husband...And a Good Dad

Chapter Six..53
Do You Want A Good Covering Or A Bad Covering?

Chapter Seven 61
Blessings And Cursings

Chapter Eight..72
Intimacy...Into Me See!

Chapter Nine 82
An Intimate Relationship With God

Chapter Ten 90
A Heritage Of "Being Tough"

Chapter Eleven..96
Do What It Takes...Not Just What You Can

Chapter Twelve 99
Today's Man

Chapter Thirteen 107
Marry A Christian Woman

Chapter Fourteen..116
Find A Christian Buddy

Chapter Fifteen..120
Our Differences Help Us Function Together

Dedication

To my children: Harry III, Roman Lee and Gabrielle Christian, who without, I would not know what true pleasure in life is. They are my treasures and the purest gift from God.

To my mother: the one who prayed when no one else knew to pray.

To my Cheryl: If I could take the pain from your life I would have no other desire. Thank you for your love of the children, your unconditional love for me and showing me the Father - Son relationship that I now have with my heavenly Father.

Acknowledgment

To Vicki Case who took my ideas, scribblings and notes and formed them into something legible and understandable.

To Cheryl who edited and corrected daily.

— CHAPTER ONE —

"THE CRISIS THAT CHANGED MY LIFE!"

It wasn't until I experienced a crisis in my life that I let down the walls I built around myself...and moved closer to God. Until this time, I thought everything was fine. From the time I married Cheryl twelve years ago, I spent most of my time and energy taking good physical and financial care of my family. But four years ago when my wife unexpectedly became ill with depression, God took off the blinders and let me see that I needed to change the way I was living.

God said, "I want you, Harry." He wanted me. He had Harry but He didn't have my heart. He wasn't my leader. He told me I didn't have to be this tough guy. I didn't have to be mad at everybody. He said, "I just want you to pull up a chair and slide next to me. Talk to me and I'll talk back to you. Whisper to me and I'll whisper back." He taught me how to care for my family in a way I never had before. This crisis was a turning point in my life.

For 8 years, I had been the Vice President of Operations of the Oral Roberts Association. I was responsible for over 1000 employees, many departments, and a large budget. I was responsible for operations, television, and was involved in many things within the ministry. I worked long hours so I left most of the spiritual rearing of our children to my wife,

Cheryl. It is difficult for me as a man to say that...but it is true. Cheryl saw to it that the children were in Sunday School. She helped them learn Bible scriptures. She taught them Christian songs. She prayed with them. I earned the living and that was that.

I knew God ordained the man to be the head of the home (Ephesians 5). I accepted this scripture at face value. I had my own version of what that meant. My interpretation was that if I put food on the table and clothes on my family's backs that was enough to be head of the home.

In the beginning, when Cheryl first became sick, I responded like a typical man. I kept saying to her, "What's wrong? What can I do to help? Go to a good doctor and get well. He can fix it and I can continue working." I was so consumed with my work at this point that I couldn't see what was happening right in front of my eyes. I kept saying to her, "We're happy. We have a good marriage. We love each other. I'm a good dad and a good husband. Why is this happening?"

Cheryl would say to different people, "Having a happy, good marriage is hard work." I would cut her right off and say, "It's not hard work for me." Now I understand what she was saying and I agree.

Then God began to show me where I was missing it. My family was the most important thing in the world to me but most of the time I wasn't with them...I was at the office.

I thought I was giving them "quality time." It didn't hit me until Lil' Harry started playing baseball. He had trouble throwing a baseball! I thought I showed him how to throw a baseball. He had a baseball. He had a glove. When he was a year and a half old, I took him to the opening day of the California Angels Athletics baseball game. I did what I thought were father and son things...but they were surface...they were not taking time with him. I showed him once. Didn't he get it? I found out that children learn by repetition and practice, over and over. Hmm...just like adults!

I remember seeing a movie called "Hook." In the movie, several corporate executives are standing at an elevator. They are all drawing their cellular telephones. One of them said to his wife, "I'm going to be late, just videotape my son's baseball game." In that moment it flashed through my mind how Cheryl had videotaped Lil' Harry at one of the Christmas musicals...that's how I watched it! I still can't believe it. I love my kids! I mean I love my kids. I tried to make time to do whatever it was with them. I should have done more than just try to make time for my children.

My cellular phone rang off the wall constantly. I would start to play golf with friends and the office would beep me 30-35 times in a round of golf it seemed. It got so my friends were enjoying my golf membership...not me. When I couldn't make it on the course they would call me. "Hey, we're having a great time...wish you were here!" That's how involved I got at work!

I was working so hard that when Cheryl got sick I handled it the way I did at the office. I went through the motions. I made decisions that were on the surface. I said, "Let me call this doctor. Let me call that doctor. I'll call Oral and he'll pray for you." These were things I could do to "fix it."

I didn't get deeply involved...until I saw my wife

start to waste away before my eyes. She drifted away and became emaciated. When she took her blouse off, you could see her ribs protruding. She started wearing turtleneck sweaters to hide the weight loss. I bought her turtleneck sweaters for Christmas...red, yellow, blue, green. I didn't want people to tell me that my wife was anorexic...because she wasn't.

Then one day Cheryl and I had a conversation that hit me hard. I remember we were standing at our kitchen counter. Cheryl choked back tears as she told me, "I just want to slip down in the bathtub or walk in the deep end of the pool and go to be with Jesus." (Cheryl wanted to leave the pain and go to be with Jesus.) I looked into her eyes and there was no one home. In that moment, I became ready to handle the problem with all the power I had in me. I said to myself, "OK. That's it. We're going to take this thing on."

As I stood at the counter, it struck me. Cheryl would do this for me...and I'm going to do this for her! My wife is dying. It was a reality in front of my eyes. Cheryl was virtually dying. It never hit me until that point. Why did she have to get to this point before I noticed it?

All of a sudden work wasn't important. I began to accompany Cheryl to the doctor. I wanted to make sure I heard the full diagnosis from the doctor. Cheryl didn't always tell me everything the doctor said. Of course, I gave her all of a sixty second commercial to tell me everything she needed to tell me from an entire day, too! I went with her to the dentist when her teeth became brittle and began to chip. I got involved with her total health.

I took care of everything from that point on. I made sure that Cheryl ate food that would help her get well. I was taking care of my boys. I was taking care of Gabrielle. I was taking care of Cheryl. I looked for the foods that had the highest fat content. It was Fetticini Alfredo. I'd go to the restaurant and pick up pizza and Fetticini Alfredo. Cheryl liked those little filet steaks with bacon wrapped around it that we had gotten at our favorite restaurant. So I found the meat market that provided them to the restaurant. I bought boxes of those steaks. I would bring them home and cook them. Then I would sit down and watch her eat. I wanted to make sure she ate the food.

I cut out coupons every Saturday. I made out the grocery list and did all the grocery shopping. I started to cook for us. I learned different ways to prepare red meat. Cheryl didn't eat red meat very often. I thought she needed more protein. I wanted to get my wife back so I started watching all the cooking shows and found new recipes for high fat food.

Cheryl had bought items for her to eat that were fat-free. (We later had a nutritionist tell us that our brains are 90% fat. Too many fat-free foods can starve your brain.) I'd go to the store and I'd load up on fat filled foods. I bought ice cream with the highest fat content. I'd go down the road and I'd say, "Let's get ice cream." Many times I brought banana splits home. I told her, "Cheryl, we have to do this." She was at the point that she would do whatever it took. Plus she was so frugal that I knew she would eat it and not waste it if I had already paid for it!

Cheryl was still ministering during this time. She was struggling to access her faith so she could receive her healing. Through the years, God healed her of many illnesses. Cheryl knew that it was important to "walk out her faith." The thing that was different this time was that she had problems "connecting" her faith because she had an imbalance in her brain that was causing her depression.

When she was on stage and under the anointing, she was a ball of fire. Then she would come home on Monday morning and she would be a corpse for three days. She drew the drapes. She didn't have the emotional energy to come out of her room. She was a walking corpse. I said, "You can't keep doing this, Cheryl." She wouldn't give up. She would say, "Well, I'm fine on stage." That's the kind of person she is...she just doesn't give up!

They asked us to do a Valentine's Day show for TBN. Cheryl's voice was raspy. In fact, she had no voice. The muscles on her neck were protruding. She wore a red dress with pearls up the neck. Then she went to do the 700 Club. She was wearing a navy blue dress. She was about 90 pounds then. Her voice was so raspy that you just wanted to clear your throat listening to her. Her fingers were all bones. All the time, I constantly pumped food into her. She was eating but wasn't getting better. She said she felt like her body was racing inside!

Time passed but Cheryl wasn't getting any better. It was discouraging. I remember going to a Thanksgiving dinner at my son Roman's school. I was there with all the other home room mothers. I thought "I'm going to raise these children alone like my mother raised me." Here's the generational curse. Here's the curse that is going to take my wife. It was an attack on my family. The first attack came when Cheryl miscarried and we lost our baby. Then there was an attack on Gabrielle. She developed sleep apnea. Next, I suffered health problems. Then Cheryl came under attack and became ill with depression. Satan struck our whole family!

Desperate for answers, I began to seek God. I prayed more...and I read and studied my Bible more. There were nights I couldn't sleep and I would go downstairs and pick up my Bible. I had always thought that God had to speak to you in some spectacular way...like he spoke to Moses from the burning bush. But I learned that God comes to me when I seek Him. Those nights He met me at the point of my need.

One night the Lord asked me, "Are you trying to control Me?" I realized that is exactly what I had been doing. I was telling Him how to do it. What I really needed was to trust God enough to get close to Him. I needed to listen to "that still small voice."

During the months of Cheryl's illness, I read about the Apostle Stephen. He was a brave man. A real man's man. He was just an ordinary guy like me. When God filled him with the Holy Spirit, he was full of power. He wasn't afraid to speak his mind. Before he died the heavens opened up. He could actually see God in heaven. When I read about Stephen, I was able to relate to him. He was a man of firm convictions. He stood alone and believed in God! That was my kind of man!

The more I searched for God, the hungrier I got to know more about Him. Cheryl and I started talking about things I found in the Bible. She would share something out of the Bible and I would read it. God would reveal things to me.   I had heard ministers preach the Word for years but *this was different.*   The Word started coming alive and I started getting personal revelation.

Four weeks after we had our conversation in our kitchen, I traveled with Richard Roberts to Zambia. When I got to Zambia, I had a lot of time to think. I missed Cheryl like I never had before. I missed the kids but I missed *her.* Cheryl and I had become very close through her dependence on me. When I traveled previously I had been able to put the distance between us on a business basis. Now God had opened my heart and made me feel tenderness that I hadn't experienced since we were first married. Both Cheryl and I could feel that God was "doing a new thing in our lives."

The Lord had shown me a Scripture in Isaiah 43:18-19 "*Do not remember the former things; neither consider the things of old. Behold, I am doing a new thing! Now it springs forth; do you not perceive and know it and will you not give heed to it?*" We needed a new thing in our lives.

Our crew went down into a copper mine and shot footage for the television program. I remember us going down...down...down. An hour and a half later, I was in the bowels of the earth. It was a hundred degrees down there. It was dark. There was sulfur and diesel fumes in the air. I was soaking wet. I have to tell you...I have a bad case of claustrophobia. My faith said I could go down into that mine...and I did! When we got down to a big dug out level I said, "OK, Richard, let's shoot our scene. This is as far as I go!"

In my frame of mind I thought I was in hell. I mean it was just hell...that's all I can say. We were in a little tunnel or cave. We went where nobody had ever gone before. They were actually digging right in front of me! I couldn't believe that men worked 12 hours a day, 7 days a week down here in this mine!

When we reached that spot, I took all the faith I had in me and said, "Father God, I am burying all the attacks of Satan against my family. I bury Cheryl's depression here beneath the bowels of the earth. I bury the abuse. I bury my dad's death. I bury *every* attack of Satan!" I thought this is the deepest point I'll ever go. These things came from the pit of hell and they had to go back there. I buried all the pain down there! In the Bible, Jesus cast the demons into the swine and drove them over the cliff. The water was a cleansing. The pain left by the time I finished my prayer. I really *believed* that I was going to have a new wife when I got back home!

We stayed in the home of the President of the Nation. When we got back to the house I couldn't wait to talk to Cheryl. I finally got a line out and I said, "Cheryl, today, while I was down in a copper mine, I buried all the attacks of Satan on our family." When I told her she wasn't sure what had happened to me. She said, "Are you OK?" She knew about my claustrophobia. I told her, "I just believed that the Lord was telling me to bury the depression. I did and I believe He is healing our family." That night I just felt the curse *lift* off my family. I knew there was something new about to happen in our lives!

When I got home, Cheryl started to get better. The weight started to come back. Her skin color was good. God led us to a Spirit-filled doctor who prayed for her and gave her medication. (The full story of

Cheryl's depression and healing can be found in the book "It's Too Soon To Give Up!) Cheryl's healing was a real miracle for our whole family!

God did not cause Cheryl's illness but He used that time to teach me things that have changed my life and the lives of my family.

During this time, I began to see what it really means to care for my family. How important it is for a man to have an intimate relationship with his Father God. I began to see my family the way God saw them.

The things that have eternal value...like loving my wife and teaching my children to walk in the love and admonition of the Lord... are now my number one priority. For years, I focused on 'material things'...things that pass away. During this crisis, I discovered what is *really* important. I learned it *wasn't things!*

My idea of what it meant to be a good husband and dad was things like putting the food on the table, putting a roof over my family's head...being a provider. I'm here to tell you...I was wrong.

It is one of the great deceptions in our society that we teach young men that being a good financial provider is the most important contribution they can make to their family. The world teaches men that they are successful if they provide well for their families. I was no exception.

I felt it was my responsibility to take physical measures to prevent bad things from happening to my wife, our children and our home. I locked the doors at night, turned on the alarm. I researched and shopped for a car that was safe for my family to ride in. I put a fire alarm in the hallway of our home...in our children's bedrooms. I checked out the coach and school system, because these people have a daily influence on the lives of my children. I accompanied my wife to the mall so she would be safe. I had outside lights for evening safety. I was attempting to prevent something bad from happening to my family by providing physical protection. I wanted to protect my family from danger...from the problems of the world.

Don't get me wrong. You should continue to make natural, physical provisions for your family. Don't stop. In fact, God will *help you* provide for the needs of your family. I seek Him every day asking for physical provisions for my family. He brings financial provision that I would never have thought of by myself. However, that's only part of what my family needs.

God opened my eyes, and for the first time in my life I saw that my earlier refusal to trust God and get close to Him had a spiritual impact on Cheryl and our children. I missed out on a lot not being spiritually connected with them. I had received my salvation but I was always "too busy" to spend time talking with them about the Lord.

I say to you, "Find the courage to get close to your Father God. Pull your chair up close to Him. He is right there in the room with you. He loves you. He wants to show you how to love and care for your family. And when the Father-God shows you how to have a strong happy family...He knows how to tell you to do it!"

— CHAPTER TWO—

"GOD HAS PROVIDED YOU WITH A SUPERNATURAL COVERING TO PROTECT YOU AND YOUR FAMILY."

God loves us so much that He has made provision for our safety in a dangerous world. When Cheryl was sick, God spoke to me as a man. He revealed that He wanted to provide something more for my family. He wanted to "cover my family" with His wings...to give us supernatural protection. At that time, I wasn't aware that God had made provision to supernaturally protect my family.

You may ask, "Why do I need protection? I've been getting along pretty well like I am." You may think that this is true. There is no doubt in my mind that you have experienced tragic situations in your life because you were living "unprotected" by God.

I discovered that my family needed protection from the daily attacks of Satan. This may be difficult to grasp but Satan generates many of the natural problems and tragedies you experience every day. The Bible says in I Peter 5:8 *"Be well balanced (sober of mind), be vigilant and cautious at all times; for that enemy of yours, the devil, roams around like a lion roaring (in fierce hunger), seeking someone to seize upon and devour."*

Every second, every minute of every day Satan is

lurking in the shadows. He never takes a vacation or takes a holiday. He never sleeps. You are human. You sleep, get weary, tired, beaten down, and discouraged, and let your natural guard down...Satan never does.

The good news is that *God is Omnipotent (all powerful, invincible, almighty). He is also Omnipresent.* He is always there. He is always on alert and knows what Satan is up to. When you invite Jesus into your life to be your personal Savior, He comes to live and work in your life. God is now your Source and your strongest Protector. He places a supernatural covering—or force field—over and around you and your wife and children.

We Christians need to place a covering over our families. If we do not take authority over Satan he will slip in as a thief in the night and cause harm to come to our loved ones.

Satan knows and trembles at this covering and hedge God places around us. In Job 1:10 Satan accuses God, *"Have You not put a hedge (covering) about him and his house and all that he has on every side? You have conferred prosperity and happiness upon him in the work of his hands, and his possessions have increased in the land."*

I always fought my own battles and provided my own protection. In the beginning, it was unfamiliar to me to try to understand and incorporate this new spiritual dimension into my life. Now that I understand the magnitude of what God has done for us, I can't imagine living any other way. It is well worth it to pray and read God's Word...to tap into this important provision. Our own efforts to protect our family from danger and from the world's problems are just plain inadequate. They aren't powerful enough.

Every day Christians are being protected by God's divine covering. I was told of a man who had prayed the covering over his son who would be flying home for the holidays. The son was about to board his plane when God told him to take another plane. The son didn't understand the Lord's direction but he had learned to be obedient. He told the airline personnel to unload his luggage. The name of the airline was Valuejet. That day the professor and his wife were watching television when they saw a news bulletin. Their son's airplane had crashed into the Florida Everglades! They were sure he was on that plane until they received a call from him. He said, "At the last minute God told me not to get on the airplane. I asked the baggage people to remove my luggage." He had not gotten on the plane! He was heartsick for the people that had boarded. He said,

"In the final minutes before the plane departed, a couple in line behind me begged the ticketing agent to get on the plane." They had boarded a plane doomed to crash!

We can fight the battle as a man in the natural...but we will never win. *There are too many things that are out of our direct control*...like the incident with Valuejet. God will fight the battle for us in the spiritual realm, but we must learn to listen to Him. We must be able to identify His Voice. When He talks to us and we must trust Him enough to obey His leading.

How can I receive God's covering in my life and the life of my family? The first thing you must do is **commit to having a personal relationship with your Father God.** You may say, 'Well, I go to church and I pray, isn't that enough?' No. God wants you to have a personal relationship with Him, a personal relationship not just being a Christian. *"And when you draw close to God, God will draw close to you."* (James 4:8) Notice who draws "close" first, first you, then God.

When I was a little boy, I lived under the same roof as my father. I lived under his authority (influence). The way I talked to him and he in turn talked with me made up our *personal relationship*. I *heard* him and he *heard* me when I talked to him. I ran to my father when I needed help. I didn't ask someone else to talk to him for me. My father always *knew* when I needed him.

Your relationship with your Father God is no different. God knows everything even if you don't tell Him. He is Omnipresent He is always there with you. Sometimes we leave Him out of our lives when we get busy. We put Him on hold...thinking we'll get back to Him later. Remember, God doesn't have an answering machine. You should talk to Him *right now!*

Once you have a personal relationship with God, you are under His authority (influence), just as we were under the influence of our natural father. Because we are under His authority, we are also under his covering (protection). Matthew 8:9

A friend of mine told me how God protected her in the eye of a tornado. It was around Christmas time, and the woman was just learning about God's protection for her family. In fact, she had just been studying the 91st Psalm and had placed a sign in her window that proclaimed *"No harm shall come nigh my dwelling."* Moments later, she turned on the radio. The radio announcer warned, "A tornado has just been spotted in East Tulsa...take cover immediately!" The location was about a block from her home. Within minutes the tornado struck. Entire walls from the homes of her neighbors flew in the air. Funnel shaped winds swirled through her front yard. There was dust and trash everywhere. There was total devastation...but although homes around her were completely demolished, her home was left untouched. She watched from her kitchen window as the tornado hovered—a block away— for 15 minutes but it never touched her home! *No harm had come near her dwelling!*

God's protection not only touches our lives it touches the lives of our family. *God's covering never leaves us or our family.* After my father died God's covering remained over our family. In Psalms 68:5 it says *God will be a covering to the fatherless and the widow.* Even when my father wasn't there to prevent things from coming against our family, God was there each new day covering us with His love. God was doing what God does...taking care of His family. God holds us in His Hand. We do not have to struggle alone trying to prevent bad things from coming against our loved ones. We now have a spiritual promise as well.

In Isaiah 51:16 it says *"And I have put My words in your mouth and have covered you with the shadow of My Hand..."* God's presence covers us with a defense of divine love and protection. Psalm 5:11 tells us, *"But let all those who take refuge and put your trust in You rejoice, because **You make a covering over them and defend them;** let those also who love your name be joyful in You and be in high spirits."*

Every morning, I place a protective covering over my wife. God gave my wife to me as a gift...it is up to me to place my covering and God's covering over her. In Genesis 2:18 *"The Lord God said, It is not good (suf-*

ficient, satisfactory) that the man should be alone; I will make him a help meet (suitable, adapted, complementary) for him...And God caused a deep sleep to fall upon Adam; and while he slept, He took one of Adam's ribs...and the rib the Lord God had taken from the man he made a woman, and He brought her to man. Then Adam said, "This creature is now bone of my bones and flesh of my flesh; she shall be called woman."

Many of us are familiar with Ephesians 5:22 that says *"Wives, be subject (be submissive and adapt yourselves) to your own husbands as (a service) to the Lord. For the husband is head of the wife as Christ is the Head of the church. Himself the Savior of (His) body..."*

God *gave* you a wife to love and comfort you. My wife is under my covering and care. She is bone of my bone and flesh of my flesh. Notice I didn't say she is under my control or domination. I said *care*. I am to love my wife as Christ loves the Church and gave His life for it. God created my wife to help-meet my needs. God created Cheryl and I to "go together"...not be separate. God wants Cheryl and I to love and enjoy each other.

Woman is virtually a part of man because she was created from the rib of man. God made the relationship between man and woman very intimate. She is ours to protect, value and love. We are to love and trust our wives.

God established marriage...not man. His plan for marriage is much richer than the world's system. Your marriage should empower and energize both of you. The Bible says that where your treasure is there will your heart be...I know that Cheryl is a treasure to me.

Now, your wife may already have a close personal

relationship with God. She may have already experienced God's protection and covering in her life. In fact, she may have been waiting and praying for you to receive your personal covering. If that is the case, let her share her knowledge of the Bible with you. Remember, God has placed you in a position of leadership in your home. A good leader makes those under him feel blessed to be under his leadership, not dominated or controlled.

When both the husband and wife have strong faith and are in agreement there is a powerful force that is born. Matthew 18:19 says, *"If two of you on earth agree (harmonize together, make a symphony together) about whatever (anything and everything) they may ask, it will come to pass and be done for them by My Father in heaven."*

If your wife doesn't know that God will cover her...or her home and children, it is your place to share this great news with her. It is best to use the carrot instead of the stick. Let her see the love Christ has placed in your heart and the many abundant provisions that are available to her. She will *see* the changes you've made in your life. She will see that God loves her and she will *want* Him in *her* life.

Your priceless children, because of your authority and relationship with God, are also under God's supernatural covering. It is up to us to train and nurture our children and teach them of God's protection. As your children grow and mature in the Lord it will become a natural thing for them to want to learn more about God's protection. They will want to place God's covering over their own lives. When you teach God's principles to your children when they are growing up it is a natural part of their existence. It is easier for them to accept Biblical teaching. If we wait until they are older to give them a foundation it becomes much more difficult to get their attention because of the negative influences of the world.

In every part of our lives we need to learn to be *conscious* and forever *thankful* for God's loving protection and covering. This is a protection that those without God do not have. God's supernatural covering keeps His children safe.

We activate our covering by saying, "Father, I ask that you cover and protect my family from all harm." When we take this action we can rest assured that God has placed a covering over our loved ones.

— CHAPTER THREE —

PROVIDER OR PARTICIPANT...
"THE TOUGH DECISION FOR MEN TODAY"

For years, I focused on being the economic provider for my family. I always had strong expectations of myself that I would provide well for my family, and that's as God planned it to be. As with many things in our lives, Satan takes things that are good and distorts them...takes them out of all balance.

Work is good at its' roots but when our work ethic causes us to continuously work excessive hours and abandon our families...it creates problems. When the *balance* between work time and home time is destroyed...there is a trail of destruction left behind. An insidious thing has happened...Satan has distorted the honorable role of provider into something that is injuring us and our families.

In a recent article entitled, *Fatherhood in the 90s,* it stated that today's young men learn one thing, "That being a good father is economic." If you bring home a paycheck or send the child support payments on time, you have fulfilled your role as a responsible father.

"What else would we expect from the world's system...no guidance, no time with the child, no striving to keep the family together." says Wade Horn, psychologist who founded the National Fatherhood Institute in Lancaster, Pa.

The article goes on to say that fatherless children are twice as likely to drop out of school. Girls who grow up in a fatherless home are far more likely to become teen mothers. Nearly 75% of American children living with single-parents will experience poverty before they turn 11. Only 20% in a two parent family will experience poverty. And last, it said that violent criminals are overwhelmingly males who grow up without fathers.

Today, children without fathers are the most at risk people in society...factoring in race, economics, neighborhoods, education or age.

When you consider families where the father is not living at home these statistics are understandable. However, what are the statistics for children who grow up in a home where the father is a workaholic? He's there *physically* but not *mentally*. And don't be deceived. You don't have to have a lot of money in order to obsess over work and money. Even men with little money can find themselves thinking about money, worrying about money—morning, noon, and night.

In the book *The Workaholic and His Family by Minirth, Meier, Wichern, Brewer and Skipper* they give a sobering picture of the success-driven male. "The most tragic result of workaholism is its effect on the family. The family of the workaholic suffers even to a greater degree than does the workaholic. The wife tries to invest herself totally in her home life or in a busy round of social activities. The failure of home life, the need for intimate emotional and physical relationship with her partner, results in anger, frustration and ultimately depression."

"The children of workaholics often experience a great inner void, a lack of identity, because of the lack of identification with one or both parents. They often talk about how their father has provided many things for them, but has never provided them with what they needed most—his time and love."

"Perhaps the most devastating effect on the children is the simple daily inoculation of the workaholic habit pattern into their lives. Also, almost as devastating is the message of conditional love: the child will be loved if he lives up to his parents' expectations. The message of conditional love should never be communicated by a father to his child. The children of a workaholic are often afraid to fail. They experience extreme anxiety even contemplating bringing home less than 100 percent on their papers."

"Many workaholics are unaware that they have any obligations (other than financial) to their homes. He leaves the responsibility for intimate relationships within the family to others. He sees no need for building the type of intimacy that is so vital to the healthy functioning of the family...No time is budgeted for the give-and-take of feelings, the discussion of emotional issues, or the handling of stresses resulting from everyday conflicts within the family. The wife must deal with all the emotional difficulties within the family on her own."

Today, just taking financial responsibility for your family is not only not enough, it can *injure* your family. Many psychologists equate workaholism with alcoholism. It does just as much damage to the family. In both cases the father is emotionally unavailable to his family most of the time.

Many men are obsessed with finances. Our young men learn this one predominant message, "The most important thing a male can do for his child is economic...to be a good provider." This message rings so loud and clear in their minds that it is hard to hear any other.

I won't deny how important it is to take care of your family financially. For goodness sake, don't stop financially providing for your family. Providing for your families is extremely important. But participating in the lives of your wife, son, daughter is far *more important*.

I had always thought it was OK to let my wife run the home as long as I put bread on the table and clothes on my families' back. If I put the money in the system I was doing my job as a father. I don't think that way anymore. I believe that men have a far greater responsibility.

I had a false sense of reality about my wife and children. A good portion of the time I didn't want to think about it. I was tired. I was discouraged. I depended on my wife to "take care of the home and children." I didn't wake up until a crisis knocked at my door...when it could have been too late to save my loved ones.

At one time I was working so hard in the ministry that I began to have symptoms of heart problems. My hair was turning gray and falling out. I was driven to do a good job. In my mind, I took on the *responsibility* for everything I touched. I thought if anything failed it was all my fault. I took the whole weight of my job and carried it on my shoulders.

At the time, I didn't understand to the level that I needed to, that I was toiling in vain to provide for my job and my family. If I had been willing to live and operate in His promises to take the cares and struggles I faced, I could have had peace in my life...even with the responsibilities. Unfortunately, I was not deeply aware of what God had done for me.

It's like the story of the immigrant family who rode in steerage coming to America. The quarters were cramped. The ventilation was bad. Many got sick. When they arrived in New York City and were ready to get off the ship they handed their ticket to the purser for verification. He looked up, surprised after reading their ticket. "Sir, you have a first class ticket. Your family could have enjoyed first class accommodations!" The family could have traveled first class but instead traveled in steerage...because they didn't know they had the right to travel first class.

In Matthew 6:33, our Heavenly Father tells us that we should *"take no thought what we shall eat or what we shall wear"* and that we should *"seek ye first the kingdom of heaven and all these things shall be added unto you."* When we learn to live in God's promises we will experience peace and love in our lives. We will give up anxiousness.

In Philippians 4:6 it says, *"Be anxious for nothing but with prayer and supplication make your needs known to God."* You change your whole quality of life when you step into God's systems, not the world's system, for meeting your needs.

Be a provider or participator? Really it should be "and" *not* "or". There should be no choice, not one or the other. We, as fathers, should be the best at both providing, AND participating!

— CHAPTER FOUR —

DO YOU WANT TO BE A FATHER OR A "DAD"?

You might think there is no difference between being a father or a dad but my life's experience tells me otherwise. There is a big gap between the two. Let me explain.

While growing up, my father was a great father to me. What I mean is he was an excellent provider. He worked six days a week. Many days he worked from 8:00 a.m. to 9:30 p.m. The only time I saw him was if my mom would take me to visit him at work. He worked through lunches, dinners, holidays, and anniversaries. He didn't think anything about it. That was his nature.

My dad had come from a long line of hard workers. Every generation before him had a strong work ethic. Even when he was a little boy his father made him work in the family grocery store instead of playing baseball in the sandlot.

While we were in church on Sunday he was outside mowing the church lawn. That was his way of doing something good for the church. It was his way of participating...and of having a relationship with God.

The son of a Lebanese immigrant, my father learned to provide for his family above all else. If he provided for his family he was a good father. His parents told him that if he wasn't financially successful he wasn't much of a man.

My father joined the Marines when the war came. He was barely 17 years old but he took pride in his self discipline and strong work ethic. Thank God for men who served in the armed forces. It shows what a strong person he was.

My father was a depression child. Work was difficult to get. People were literally starving in the streets. You worked whenever you could and wherever you could and as long as they would let you.

My mom was very understanding. They both did what they thought was right and necessary for the family. He didn't work hard because he wanted to hurt his children. He definitely didn't work hard because he didn't care. He did it to provide for his family. His background contributed to him being a great father (provider) but a lousy dad (participant).

He was so busy working hard that he didn't hear that still small voice that wanted to guide his life...that voice that wanted to tell him how to function according to God's way...not his.

You might be thinking "What is so bad about a man who wants to provide the best for his family?" Nothing. But that's not enough. You see I wish my father could have understood this one thing. I needed him to have an intimate relationship with me more than to give me toys. I would have much rather had him be home with me playing catch with an old baseball glove. I wanted him with me. I didn't like playing ball against the side of the house alone while he was out working to buy me that new baseball glove.

My father was a workaholic. A workaholic is the same as an alcoholic...they both have an addictive spirit. That spirit is a deception of Satan. He tells us that the way to happiness is through things.

Satan has been lying to us about our work lives. He deceives us into believing that if we aren't working day and night to achieve status or gain money that our families will do without. The truth is we need to work to support our families but we need to be conscious of having a balance in our lives.

I want you to know I had the utmost respect for my father and loved him immensely. However, this cycle of workaholism has to stop, especially for my family and now maybe yours.

There is a movie called *The Electric Light Horseman*. The man in a scene asks to have the room cleared. There was a problem but no one knew how to address it. One of the men got up and went to the bar. He turned and said, "Ah, the world of illusion."

That is a perfect description of the world Satan likes to show us. It is smoke and mirrors. It is an illusion. He deceives us into believing lies...telling us that we must work hard and leave the family to the wife. He deceives us into believing that by drinking alcohol we can get some false feeling that will make it easier to communicate with people in a tense situation. He tells workaholics that it's normal to work hard. You must work this hard in your job to be respected. It is the *only* way to provide what your family needs.

I worked hard, just like my father, until our family hit a wall of crisis. Unfortunately, it took a crisis to get my attention and let me see how vulnerable our family could be without my taking the spiritual leadership of my family.

At 26 years old I was the Vice-President of the Oral Roberts Evangelistic Association, Vice-President of buildings and the grounds and head of Oral Roberts television. I was responsible for 1000 employees. I became so stressed that I developed heart problems. I didn't realize it but I was walking in my father's footsteps, Cats In The Cradle.

I might have gone on that way but a crisis definitely got my attention. God didn't cause our crisis Satan did. I left us uncovered and Satan came running in as the destroyer that he is. But God took the problem, the curse, the attacks and He turned it into a blessing for us. He helped me take some giant steps through the crisis and grow in Him on my way to the other side.

When Cheryl was pregnant with our fourth child she threatened to miscarry. I was home in Tulsa and Cheryl was in the Dallas airport. She had hemorrhaged while in the airport. They rushed her by ambulance to Northridge Hospital. They patched in the police radio from the ambulance to call me. "Your wife is hemorrhaging and we don't know why. Get here." I didn't even get a chance to tell them she was pregnant.

I rushed to the hospital in Dallas. All the way Satan whispered to me, "You're going to lose your wife. You're going to lose this baby.

Your boys will lose their mother. You will have to raise your two boys by yourself. You'll be a single parent just like your mother."

When I walked into her hospital room my wife was sitting up on the edge of the bed preaching. I *saw* her faith but where was *my* faith? Her faith had brought her through a car crash. She went through a windshield. The engine came in and crushed her leg and crippled her. She had over a hundred stitches in her face. Today, there are no visible scars. She can walk because Jesus healed her. Her faith said she wasn't going to let Satan steal her dream. She sought God for her healing and today she stands before us as a former Miss America, healed and whole.

Cheryl's faith was a hard thing to take as a man. I thought, "Your wife stood alone as a little girl and she is standing alone right now. *Man, where is your faith?* You work for Oral Roberts. You're supposed to have faith." It started working on me. Sometimes those of us in the ministry know the Word, we breathe the Word, we speak the Word, we give the Word to others but we lack getting close to God.

The doctors thought we had lost the baby but God miraculously saved our little Gabrielle. They did tell us that Cheryl would have to be bedfast for over seven months. That was a real challenge. Keeping Cheryl in bed was somewhat like trying to cage King Kong!

Cheryl had never had to be dependent on anyone and it was difficult. When Little Gabrielle was born we breathed a sigh of relief. We were sure that we had received our miracle and could go on with our lives. It didn't happen that way. Satan launched a major attack on our family.

After Gabrielle was born she developed sleep apnea. This is where the baby can die without warning in their sleep...they just stop breathing. It has been known to cause crib death. Cheryl slept with Gabrielle right by her bed...for months she never got more than 15 minutes of sleep at a time.

Gabrielle got better but Cheryl fell into a deep depression. I would ask her what was wrong so I could fix it. She would tell me "If I knew, I would fix it. I just feel like whoever is in this body is not me. I feel like I'm no earthly good to anyone here."

My wife, who had been our spiritual leader, had become completely dependent on me. In Matthew 6:21, it says, *"Where your treasure is, there will your heart be."* I knew Cheryl was my treasure. I knew that it was up to me to battle Satan's attack on our family.

I started changing. I did everything I knew to do spiritually. I read my Bible. I started reading Christian articles. I started talking to people. I started listening, not just watching Christian TV. I started listening to what God was telling me inside. I would pray. The children would pray. We would pray together to put a spiritual cover over her.

Cheryl and I started talking more and reading our Bible together. Cheryl had always wanted that but I had felt pressured to do something I wasn't ready for. She wanted a partner in the Word. She liked to dig through Scripture...I wanted surface. Scrape off the top and you've got me down. Most men won't take the top layer off. I needed that top layer removed.

God began scraping the top off by directing me to a church service on Father's Day. The pastor talked about a father being faithful...about providing *and* participating. I wrote it all down. Then I saw a program about children and families on TV. The commentator said that parents can impact their children...or have them close...for a short time. When they are young they are hungry for your closeness in their lives. If they don't get that closeness when they're young, they won't want you or have room for you in their lives when they're older. That hit me like a ton of bricks! It was a revelation.

I had been seeking God for answers and He was

talking to me loud and clear! I knew I had been a good provider but I was not participating in the lives of my children. I began to hear the Lord talking to me. He said, "I want you, Harry." I thought, "He *wants* me!" He had Harry but He didn't have my heart.

I had been waiting for this big sign from God. I wanted the clouds to open up...lightening to strike. I wanted a burning bush. But God was speaking to me with that powerful "still small voice."

The more I sought God the more I found comfort in the Father- Son relationship I was having with Him. He asked me to sit quietly with the TV off...to pull up a chair and sit next to Him and talk. He asked me to tell Him my problems. He wanted to comfort me. He knew all about my problems. He just wanted me to rest in Him and let Him carry my burdens.

I knew God would much rather I spent time with Him every day, getting to know Him and His way of doing things, building a relationship with Him, than always being too busy with work, TV, or the newspaper.

I asked myself, "Do I read the Bible or sit and communicate with God at least as long as I read the newspaper each day? Do I spend as much time with Him as I do watching sports on TV? Do I pray as long as I watch TV at night? Think about it, Harry." I didn't have to think about it...I knew the answer. It was "no."

Through faith, prayer and a Spirit-filled doctor, Cheryl recovered from the devastating depression. God had worked a miracle in our lives. He had helped us pull together as a family. He showed me the importance of having a covering over our family at all times. He showed me what it means to be the real head of the house and have an intimate relationship with my wife and my children.

I discovered one way to spend quiet time with God is on my way to work. I'm alone. No radio on. I just tell Him what I'm feeling that day...what I need. I thank Him for the many blessings He has given me. It is the time I take to place a prayer covering over all my family for that day.

Some of you may be thinking, "Some fathers have to work all these hours to make ends meet." Fair statement. Especially today with the high cost of living...and the demands put on fathers and mothers are many. Your child asks, "Why can't I have a new video game? Johnny has one." Sound familiar?

That's tough because by nature we want our children to have what other children have...if not more. These situations are a perfect way to instill values in our children. We need to help our children have a clear understanding of what is really valuable...and what is not.

Children are very perceptive and it won't take them long to understand that *people* are more important than *things*. It can be surprising to find out what is important to them anyway.

One father talks about buying expensive Christmas presents for his children only to watch in disbelief while they shoved the expensive presents in the corner and sat playing with a ribbon from the packages!

Once we do our job correctly...raising our children to see what is really valuable...we can expect them to be understanding and caring beyond belief. Values are what drive people to do what they do...having the right values is more precious than goals, money or possessions.

I know kids can be demanding of fathers and mothers...but if we instill in them the importance of having a personal relationship with their parents—and how it is possible to lose those close relationships when financial pressures become too great—I believe our children will understand. I have faith that they will not only understand but want their time with their loved ones over that new baseball glove or Nintendo.

There were two people looking at a friend's headstone. It struck them both that the dash mark between the birth date and the death date represents a person's life...in just a little dash mark. A man's whole life was represented in that mark! The person may have been blessed of the Lord. Or his dash mark could represent a man who spent his whole life working from sun up to sun down...and his family may have never gotten to know him. In the end, it is much more important to know the impact of his love during his lifetime than what possessions he may have had. Memories of his lifetime are more important than his bank balance.

Motivational Speaker, *Tony Robbins*, says that if you want to really know how important something is in your life...give it the *rocking chair test*. Imagine yourself when you are old sitting in your rocking chair on the front porch, reflecting back over your life. Will you be saying "I'm thankful that I took time to be with my family" or will you say, "I wish I could have spent more time with my wife and children. I don't feel close to them at all."

Pretty sobering thought, isn't it? But it's not too late. It's Christmas morning. In the beloved Christmas Story of Ebineezer Scrooge...even though he had made mistakes in his life...Ebineezer received a second chance to make things right. We have that opportunity too.

If you have lost your father the way I lost mine you may be thinking the same way I do. My father was a great provider but I don't have many memories of him with me. Yes, I have memories, but not father son memories. I would trade anything he ever gave me to have another father son memory with him. I know it's easy to say that now and that it might not have been that easy when I was a little boy and really wanting a new baseball glove but I believe I would have wanted dad around more than I did that glove.

Make sure the dash mark on your headstone represents the times and memories your loved ones had with you. Don't let it represent that during your whole lifetime you didn't spend periods of time with them. Don't let it represent that the only memories they have of you is working!

— CHAPTER FIVE —

HOW TO BECOME A GOOD HUSBAND... AND A GOOD DAD

If you want to become the best husband and dad you're capable of...you can. Begin right now! It's simple. You don't have to quit your job or go through some drastic changes. You can start today. There are just a few things that you need to rethink and retrain yourself to do.

The first, most important thing I had to come to grips with in my own life was, **deciding to change.** I was thankful that God showed me how important it was to become closer to my family. But nothing would have happened if I hadn't made *a decision that I absolutely had to change.*

It would have never happened without me being truly motivated to change. Experts say that true change will not happen until a person is extremely uncomfortable with the way his life is at present. If we're comfortable we tend to stay that way. In my case I was both comfortable...and uncomfortable. I was definitely unhappy and unfulfilled having Cheryl take over the spiritual leadership of our kids. I knew she was doing what I should be doing. But I was comfortable not having to make the effort to change. I think it's a dilemma many men face.

There were several things that motivated me to

change. For all the years of my marriage I had watched
Cheryl do the things I should have been doing with our
kids. Although I never talked to anyone about it...it
bothered me. It wasn't Cheryl's fault. She stepped in
to cover for me. I worked a lot and when I was home
I didn't do spiritual things. I knew that the Bible said
that a man should perform certain spiritual duties...but
I didn't do them. I knew I needed to change but I did-
n't know quite how.

One of the problems I had was that Cheryl did such
a good job providing spiritual covering for our family it
was easy to let her continue to do it. At the time, I
read my newspaper and watched sports on TV. *I did-
n't have a strong enough reason to change.*

What I didn't realize is that I was missing out on
some very special times with my family. It wasn't until
I started investing time being with my family that I
developed a rich, intimate relationship with them.
Since that time, I have found that there are great
rewards in developing that kind of connection. The
more time I spend with them the better I get to know
them. I get to experience on a deep level, what is happening with each of my children.

No one can understand why I cut my boy's hair.
They say, "Why on earth are you cutting their hair?" I
tell them, "I want to spend time with my boys. I want
to play an active role in their lives. The most intimate
time a father can have with his son is when he's cutting
his hair. He'll remember that."

There is a quotation that says, "At three, dad is the
world; at five dad is my best friend; at eight, dad's great;
at ten, dad's all right; at fifteen, dad's not cool any
more; at eighteen dad's out of touch; at twenty one,

dad's lost his mind; at thirty, dad's cool again; at forty, I should ask dad; at forty-five, I'd better ask dad first; at fifty, I wish dad, my best friend, was around so we could just talk."

I lost my father when I was 10 years old so I lost out on that father-son relationship. I don't want to let that happen with my kids. Now, I want to be the most involved father at my kid's school. I'm at their Tai-Kwon-Do matches. I'm at their baseball games. I coach their basketball team. These activities have been more rewarding to me than I can tell you.

When there is a problem at school my child confides in me. He asks "What should I do? There is a bully at school who always teases me." This is a special father-son moment. Cheryl might not agree with my solutions to the problems but the time I spend with my children is an investment in our future relationship.

When they are adults they won't want to shut me out of their lives. Guiding my child makes me feel that connection that God intended me to have with my children. I also get to share in the innocent humorous things my children say and do.

The biggest motivation I had to change was when Cheryl became ill. During her illness I *couldn't* continue running my life the way I had before. When I changed things began to change in my family.

Several things happened. **First**, God helped me rise to the occasion to care for my family. It was as if I had supernatural strength to accomplish the task. Our family was forced to learn how to function without Cheryl's strength. That sounds simple, but when you change the role of a strong person in your family structure, it's a challenge. At that time in our lives everyone was depending on me. Cheryl depended on me. The children depended on me. I had to take care of many of the physical needs we had. I didn't understand how to do that...but I gave it everything I had. When I rolled up my sleeves and got more involved with my family, God worked a miracle. Even though this was a difficult time...it was a good time for our family. What Satan meant for bad God actually turned around for our good.

Second, God helped me see how great it was to get close to my wife and family. I really enjoyed being on the front line of family life. *I realized that the most important things in my life...where my treasure is...are my wife and family.* When Cheryl got better I didn't want to go back to the way things had been before. I didn't want to go back to experiencing the distance—when I was spending so much time at work—that we had all felt before Cheryl's illness.

Third, I understood for the first time the *importance* of the man taking leadership in the home. A woman can function in this role if she is forced to...but the role does not perfectly fit her as God planned. God ordained the man to be the spiritual leader in the home and it is a perfect fit. There are some things that God meant only for a man to do. God meant for the man to place a spiritual covering over his wife and children on a daily basis. He also meant for the dad to teach the wife and children how to put a covering over themselves. If we leave our loved ones spiritually uncovered they are fair game for Satan's attacks.

I used to think that taking spiritual leadership in the home was some awesome, overwhelming task. It's not. The reason that it is not is because God is right there with you each step of the way. Here's how it works. All you have to do is develop a personal relationship with your Father God and read your Bible. God will guide you every step of the way. You trust God to be God and then you give Him place in your life and then in your family.

So make up your mind to change...and start. I think it's very important to have strong reasons to change or chances are you won't try. Not having good reasons to become a good husband and father...do not equal change! If you say, "Harry, I don't have a strong reason to change. My situation is different that yours was."...Stop. Take time to get in touch with the real situation here. Get a very clear picture in your mind of what could happen to you and your family if you don't change...if you don't take action.

Imagine your wife totally disconnected from you. You're like acquaintances who move distantly through life. Or you're like the couples you see in restaurants who have a dead look on their faces and don't talk to each other.

You don't have any of the juice or joy for your life together...you've lost your passion. This is one of the reasons the divorce statistics are so high...people allow themselves to drift apart. I think Satan likes it when we destroy our own relationships through apathy, I just don't care anymore.

How will this kind of marriage impact your children? What will happen if you don't teach them about the Lord? They will be no match for the destructive things they will face in life. If you aren't spending quality time *and* quantity time with them, you will not be a part of their lives, they will always go to their mother when they have a need.

I learned if you aren't close to your children and spending time with them when they are young, don't count on them allowing you into their lives when they are older. Lastly, and more importantly, society can't teach your son how to be a man as good as you can. That job is up to you. Children don't do what we say. They do, what we do.

So, **decide** that you're going to change. Make up your mind that you *want* to change. Make a quality decision that this is a life and death decision...the life or death of your family! If you don't make that positive decision you will plod along, you will try, and you will fail.

Ask a person who has lost a lot of weight on a diet. "Why did this diet work when the others failed?" Almost without exception they'll say, "I finally found a diet that worked and I knew that this was my *last chance* to get rid of the weight. I just made up my mind that it was time to lose this weight." They made a *decision* and they made a total lasting change in their eating and exercise way of life. *You have to decide to stand for something or you will fall for anything.*

Stand up as a man for your family. People will do much more to keep from losing something than they will to gain something. Losing your family could definitely be an irreplaceable loss...one you will regret for the rest of your life.

After you've made the decision that your wife and family are valuable to you...**start now**. The journey of a thousand miles begins with the first step.

Remember your actions don't have to be perfect. Satan may be telling you that you have to do everything perfect. He tells you that you should never attempt anything unless you can do a perfect job. That's a lie of the devil. When you're first learning to do something it won't be perfect at first. With each new experience you will grow. *There is no such thing as failure...only experience.* You learn what doesn't work and you try again. Only this time you have more information. The important thing is to take action. Do something.

Develop a plan of action. In life, "If you don't plan...you plan to fail." In business "You plan your work and work your plan." This is the way you accomplish things. Your home life shouldn't be any different. You *schedule* your time to meet the needs of your employer or employees. You are *habitual* in many of the things you do at work. Have you ever asked yourself, "How much is a good habit worth?" I can tell you it's worth a lot.

Why not develop *spiritual habits* that will get you closer to your family? Read the Bible together...pray...talk about spiritual issues. Faith without works is dead. Get up. Exercise. Do something. Get a plan of action just as you do at work and stick with it.

Make a decision to *habitually* plan time to spend with each member of your family. Susannah Wesley had 27 children and she spent special time with each of them every day! When she wanted time alone she signaled her children by putting her apron over her head.

So set a schedule. Every day I will spend time talking with my wife. We will discuss challenges that each of us face...things we're discouraged about as well as our joys. We'll read the Bible together. Even a few verses will make a difference.

Schedule time with the children right after you finish the evening meal. Ask them the kind of questions that do not elicit superficial answers. If you want to know what's going on in your children's lives you have to dig deep.

Make them feel comfortable with you by not using this time to be judgmental.

When it is necessary to discipline, help them understand that you want to be fair. Give them a good explanation for the decisions you make. Take turns reading from the Bible. Learn to talk about God frequently...as a natural, normal part of life. God doesn't just live in church...He lives in our homes if we invite Him, into our heart and our home!

Only *you* can make time for your children. You know there is only a short window of opportunity that you will have with your child. Don't miss that window. Your children will reach an age when their friends are more important to them than you will be. You will have missed the window where you were the most important person to them. Don't let it slip by.

There are days when you will feel as if you haven't done all you could have. Remember, an action, no matter how small, is extremely valuable in the eyes of your family...and the Lord. *Take baby steps at first.* It takes 21 days to develop a new habit. Once it becomes a habit you won't have to consciously think about it anymore.

The first time you try to do something, it feels unfamiliar and awkward. Remember, the first time you attempted to play football or bowl? You weren't born with a football in your hands but you learned how to play. Do you *think* about combing your hair or brushing your teeth? Of course not. Once it becomes a habit to be intimate with your family, it will come quite naturally.

I found that it helped me to **prioritize my life.** I had to consciously ask myself what was most important to me. Was it reading the newspaper, watching sports on TV or passing out in the recliner at the end of the day? Those things gave me personal pleasure and were important for my relaxation but they didn't necessarily help my family.

It has been my experience that God will bless us and our families when we get our priorities right. *God wants us to put Him first in our lives.* In Matthew 5:6 it says, *"Blessed are those who hunger and thirst for righteousness sake for they shall be filled."* When you are *"hungry"* for the things of God, you change your focus and in turn your values. Your values are no longer open to compromise. You develop integrity.

I have always been a goal setter. An important part of goal setting is setting strong priorities. Setting goals is a good thing to do. I strive to be the best person I can be. God wants me to provide well for my family. It is important to remember, however, not to get your priorities in the wrong place. **"Don't let the goals you set compromise your values, or the things that are important to you!"**

I believe God will bless my family when I **get my priorities right.** I believe that God wants me to have integrity. *"A good name is rather to be chosen than great riches, and loving favor rather than silver or gold."* (Proverbs 22:1) And *"Blessed are those who hunger for righteousness for they shall be filled."* (Matthew 5:6)

Once I establish that my values are without compromise...that I hold my values to be extremely important in my life...my achievements will go far beyond what they ever were before. Anyone can set a goal. When I make sure that my goals have integrity, they will far exceed prior accomplishments. They will be as gold or silver.

My spiritual goals are more rewarding than anything

that is purely an earthly goal. God's way is to have integrity and values. If you don't believe it, just check out the Ten Commandments. Think about it. We are not to steal, covet another man's things or commit adultery. These are qualities that make a Godly man...not a man of this world.

A good set of values starts with **Valuing your relationship with God.** Thank Him for what He has done for you. When I started developing an *attitude of gratitude* it helped me remember the many things He has done for my family. When you place a high value on anything you will give it high priority.

Value **your wife.** The Bible says she is "flesh of your flesh." Do you want your wife to value you? Then value her. Love and appreciate her.

Value **your children.** They are a gift from God. God has entrusted them to you. They are your seed and a reflection of you. In the future, they will be responsible for spreading the gospel around the world.

Value **your job**...your work or ministry. What you do for a livelihood establishes your monetary worth in this world and it helps you provide for your family. So do your best. Make sure your job is fulfilling because it will make it more enjoyable to you and it will help you do a better job.

Value **giving.** This is one of the most important things to value. It is from your giving, tithing, or charity work that you will receive from God. Your blessings from God are directly in proportion to your giving. God loves a cheerful giver. He will multiply your seed sown (some thirty, some sixty, some one hundred times). It's God's law. You can't outgive God.

I found that in order to change the way I had been

doing things, I had to decide what things were important to me and give them priority. It helped me when I placed priorities on things before they happened. *If you make a decision before the situation occurs you will be more likely to stick to the things that have value to you.*

For instance, if I have already decided that my wife has a high priority in my life, I will stop what I am doing to talk to her when she needs me. I will give her my time *first.* I will not wait until it is convenient for me to talk to her.

Have you ever stopped to think what has the biggest priorities in your life? Is it a priority to sit in front of your television set? Is it important to your family for you to sit on the couch and vegetate and get fat? What are your priorities? Is it important for you to travel? Do you want to spend most of your free time with friends? Or is it a priority for you to spend time with your family? Who can *you* influence more, your friends or your family?

Some people talk about what they would do if they had just one more day on earth...or another chance. It's like when you played baseball and struck out when it was your turn to bat. It wasn't perfect and you thought to yourself *"If I could only take my turn over." Many times we don't get "to take our turn over" with our families.* As kids we called it a "do over." Start a "do over" with your family.

I once heard a college student say that there was never enough time in the day. What she may not have understood is we all have the same amount of time...but we use our time differently. *We spend our time on the things that have the biggest priorities in our lives.*

When you're in college you definitely have to put priorities on where you spend your time. It's sometimes hard for a student to believe but they have more time as a single college age student than they will as a working parent. **You have to *make time* for the priorities in life.** The priorities in life are God, family and after that it is up to you.

Scott O'Grady, a young American pilot who was shot down behind enemy lines said, "My priorities weren't turned around in Bosnia. I'd been re-examining them for quite some time. They came into line during that first week in June. By the end of that time, I realized that only three things mattered in this world. *First*, was faith in God, the Source of all goodness. *Second* was the love of family and friends. That love wasn't something apart from faith...it wasn't a by product...it was faith's fullest expression. *Third*, was good health...the physical foundation for faith and love. Beyond that, everything was negotiable."

There is a quotation that I think is very true. "Never sweat the small stuff...and almost everything *is* small stuff."

— CHAPTER SIX —

"DO YOU WANT A GOOD COVERING...OR A BAD COVERING OVER YOUR HOME?

Most men don't understand what it means to have a spiritual covering over their home. They aren't aware of its' existence. Maybe the best way to explain it is to go to the illustrations given in Scripture.

Deuteronomy 33:12 *"The beloved of the Lord shall dwell in the safety by Him, and the Lord shall cover Him all the day long, and He shall dwell between his shoulders."*

Psalm 91:4 *"He shall cover thee with His feathers, and under His wings shall thou trust, his truth shall be thy shield and buckle."*

These scriptures tell us that we can have a **good covering over our homes**. They help us understand the value of having a good covering over our home. Here's how having a good covering saved my wife and possibly my children's lives.

Several weeks before our second child Roman Lee was born, God woke Cheryl up. God said, "Go anoint all of your doors and all of your windows. Put a hedge of protection...a prayer cover over all your family." She thought it was strange because she had done that earlier but she had learned through the years to be obedient to God's voice.

Three weeks later our second child Roman Lee was born. I was still high from all the excitement when I received a telephone call from the police. Roman was only one day old. They wanted me to come down to the station. At the station they asked, "Do any of these women look familiar?" I couldn't believe my eyes. "Yes, they all look like my wife. They are all brunettes. They're all about 30 years old. They're all about 5'7" tall. And that happens to be my wife and that is our office address." The sergeant, seeing the shocked look on my face, explained, "We have arrested a stalker who abducted two women...and so forth. Your wife was next on his list."

The question is "Why not Cheryl? Why didn't he abduct her?"

My wife is more publicly known than the other women in the man's notebook and it would have been natural for him to abduct her first.

The reason was that God told Cheryl to place a covering over our home. At that time in our lives, I had not realized the importance of the covering. I did not know about this protection. But Cheryl did. You will never convince Cheryl and me that God did not protect her.

God had placed a supernatural covering over Cheryl and our then unborn son Roman. He held Cheryl in the palm of His Hand. He created a "hedge of protection" around our home to protect Cheryl and Roman from the snares of Satan and his demons.

There is also a **bad covering.** Let's look at the Scriptures that explain it.

Job 26:6 *"Hell is naked before him, and destruction hath no covering."*

Isaiah 30:1 *"Woe to the rebellious children, saith the Lord, that take counsel, but not of me, and that cover with a covering, but not of my spirit, that they may add sin to sin."*

Obadiah 1:10 *"For thy violence against thy brother Jacob shame shall cover thee, and thou shall be cut off forever."*

It is important to understand that if you do not cover your home and family with a good covering...a bad covering will eventually seek them out and cover them. There is either a good covering or a bad covering placed on your family. It is up to you.

God is the One who places a good covering on the man. Man is covered by God. The man covers his wife and children. There is a line of authority.

In this day and age there isn't a lot of respect paid to authority. Many people scoff at authority. There's a humorous saying that helps you understand the power of authority in the home. "If mama ain't happy, ain't nobody happy." What that is saying is that "Mama sets the tone of the home." However, dad also sets the tone of the house and home. Dad sets the covering. If dad ain't covered nobody is covered. See the similarity.

The exception to this is when a woman's husband isn't walking with the Lord. She can cover herself, her husband and her children until he gets saved.

The good or bad covering over the house sets the stage for what goes on inside and outside the house. *The covering you have over your home determines your authority over things that go on in and around your home.*

The good covering gives you spiritual authority. You have authority over your family and friends that come in contact with you or come into your house.

The covering sets your proper God-given authority over Satan. *We have authority over Satan if we take it and use it.* Take authority over the devil. Place your covering of protection under God and over your family because then Satan has no authority over your house. You have to realize that you can trust God to protect you and your family. No man is bigger or better than God. We must first trust Him!

When your family does not have a good covering over them, they have a bad covering. They are *unprotected.* Once you have a bad covering you and your family will come under the attack of Satan. You can count on it.

Satan will infiltrate your home with the wrong type of friends for your children. They will bring in unclean spirits with them. He can gain entrance and thieves will come to steal from you. He may come in through the television cartoons your children watch. Today, many cartoons are purely satanic and full of witchcraft. Some contain so-called "harmless spells." Don't you ever believe there is such a thing as "Harmless spells."!

*One of the strategies that Satan uses most often is to catch us off guard...*to make a surprise attack. Satan sent a stalker to attack my wife when she was at a very vulnerable place. She was nine months pregnant. Our thoughts were on the miracle of having a baby. We were expecting good things to come. She was not expecting this attack. I was not expecting a mad man to accost my wife! I mean, who in their right mind thinks that someone wants to kill their loved ones. That is why we need to place a good spiritual covering over our family at all times.

There are too many examples of Satan's surprise

attacks. Not long ago, a group of teenagers bludgeoned a couple to death. The teenagers were practicing vampire worship and often drank each other's blood. One girl in the group was the granddaughter of an official in an international ministry. It was also her parents that the teenagers beat to death.

Friends said that the girl fell in with the wrong crowd four years ago, when she was only 13 years old. It wasn't long before she became part of the cult. The grandfather said she was always quiet and that he never saw the brutality coming!

We must also be sensitive to the urging of the Holy Spirit. When we feel a leading to take action we must not hesitate. There might have been a disastrous outcome if Cheryl had not been obedient to the Holy Spirit and gotten out of her comfortable bed to anoint the windows and doors. When God woke Cheryl up and told her to place a prayer cover over our home she immediately did what she was told to do. Why wasn't the stalker successful? He wasn't successful because of a strong defense God had placed around our home.

Satan wanted to attack Cheryl because of the strong anointing she has on her life. He wanted to kill her. Satan sent a demonic attack to assassinate our lives, to kill without remorse or reason. He wanted to destroy my wife and my family and destroy our happiness. Thank God for the covering and Cheryl's obedience.

In 1977, there was a Christian mother who prayed for her grown son who was about to leave on a business trip. She prayed and placed a covering over him for a safe flight. While the two of them prayed together she unexpectedly began to weep. Her son said it was the first time he had ever seen his mother cry.

As it turned out, there was a reason for the tears. Later that day her son was in one of the worst accidents in aviation history! There were two planes poised on the runway for take off. One aircraft did not wait for clearance and the two airplanes collided just over the runway as they both became airborne. There were over 500 people killed in the accident. The son yelled amid the carnage, "I stand on the Word. In the name of Jesus I am safe." Due to his active faith...and the covering that was placed over him by his mother...he walked away from the aircraft without a scratch!

We must remember to place a prayer covering over our families at all times. Every day and every night our children should put on the whole armor of God. Every day and every night our children are under attack. I place a covering over them...and they place their own personal covering over themselves. It is a visible witness before God and against Satan.

We have taught them that there is bad in the world and there is good...and they know how to fight the devil. They are aware of the evil that is out there and they understand that they are to avoid it at all cost. Whether they turn on the television set and see something that is demonic, or if they are in school and someone comes up to them with something not allowed in their lives...they know how to deal with it.

It is never too early to start teaching your children right from wrong or the difference between good and evil. Deuteronomy 11:18 *"So keep these commandments carefully in mind. Tie them to your hand to remind you to obey them, and tie them to your forehead between your eyes! Teach them to your children. Talk about them when you are sitting at home, when you are walking, at bedtime and before breakfast! Write them upon the doors of your houses and upon your gates, so that as long as there is sky above the earth, you and your children will enjoy the good life awaiting you in the land the Lord has promised you."*

When we follow God's instructions for our children we are teaching them to be close to God and we teach them how to spiritually protect themselves. Today, many children in the world are defenseless because parents didn't take the responsibility teaching their children about the Lord.

If you did not teach your children about the Lord and His covering when they were young...it is never too late! *Your church may not have taught you about the covering.* You can still pray for them and talk to them about the Lord. You can teach them about the covering. If you were not a Christian when they were young, they have an opportunity to see the changes you have made in your life. It *will* have an impact on them.

The world places coverings over their investments to protect them. When you construct a house it is essential that you put on a good, solid roof. I don't care how much time you spend rebuilding, reconstructing the inside of an old house to make it look good...you need to have a twenty-five year roof. Why? For protection...to protect your investment...to protect the things you value...to protect what you spent your hard earned money on...what you labored for with your time and sweat. A new roof. A covering. Get it?

Even a contractor puts a good reliable covering over his investment, his treasure. He generally has a guarantee or a warranty. *Why do we treat our family worse than a building? "Where your treasure is there is your heart."* (Matthew 6:21) Isn't your family your treasure? Then that is where your heart should be. God is the author of the first and best guarantee. He will cover and guarantee protection for your home if you let Him.

— CHAPTER SEVEN —

BLESSINGS AND CURSINGS

Blessings

Luke 1:50 *"And His mercy (His compassion and kindness) is on those who fear Him with godly reverence, from generation to generation and age to age."*

Genesis 12:3 *"And I will bless those who bless you (confer prosperity or happiness upon you) and curse him who curses or uses insolent language toward you..."*

Psalm 5:11 *"But let all those who take refuge and put their trust in You rejoice; let them ever sing and shout for joy, because You make a covering over them and defend them; let those who love Your name be joyful in You and be in high spirits."*

Deuteronomy 23:5 *"...and the Lord your God turned the curse into a blessing to you, because the Lord your God loves you."*

Cursings

I Kings 15:3 *"He walked in all the sins of his father before him; and his heart was not blameless with the Lord his God.."*

I Kings 14:18 *"...visiting the sins of the fathers upon the children, upon the third and fourth generation."*

For years, medical researchers have told us that the tendency to have certain diseases can be transmitted from generation to generation. It is true that certain families...unless they believe God for their divine healing and health...seem to have heart problems...or cancer...or other diseases. When you go to get a medical check up, the first thing the doctor asks is "Did your parents and grandparents experience recurring diseases?" Spirit-filled doctors use this information to effectively fight disease that is attacking your body. Thank God for Spirit-filled doctors!

Today, taking a health history is such common procedure we don't even think about it when doctors ask us these questions. Years ago, many doctors and researchers did not understand that the tendency to have certain disease was passed from generation to generation. Countless people perished because we didn't understand the implications of generational diseases. That has all changed. Today, we know that certain diseases can reoccur in families. Lives are being saved with this information. (If you have a family history that concerns you then you must bind the devil in the name of Jesus and claim God's divine health.)

Today, we are discovering a wealth of new information regarding emotional and social problems. We now know that the tendency toward alcoholism, co-dependency, food addictions, and physical abuse can be passed from generation to generation. Many of the people who suffered from sick parents pass it on to the next generation. Thank God there is a definite movement today to stop this dysfunction from being passed on to the next generation. If there is dysfunction in your family make a decision that it will stop with your generation!

I was ignorant in this area until I started dealing with abuse in people's lives. I started asking questions. "Why does it happen? Where did it come from? Who could do something bad to people they love?"

Cheryl always says some good people have bad problems. But it goes much deeper than that. Good families can have bad problems, problems and curses. Think about it. There are some families where everything they touch turns out great. There are other families where tragedy abounds.

You can generally trace a families' history—good or bad—back to a specific person or incident. If you think about it, in the Old Testament God warned the Israelites to stay away from their idolatrous neighbors because He knew the impact it would have on their lives. When you live with people who have sin in their lives—those who worship the gods of money, alcohol or sex—it can impact you and your descendants for generations to come.   This is a pretty sobering thought...but it's the truth. Don't make the mistake of letting sin into your life and home. You can have disastrous results!

In II Corinthians 6:14 it says, *"Don't be unequally yoked"* for this reason. You cannot casually introduce a non-Christian into your family through marriage without impacting future generations.

When a curse enters a family tree it doesn't just impact that family...it passes from generation to generation. The people in the families often don't realize what has happened historically. They ask, "Why are these bad things always happening to us?"

What you may not realize is that you are in a spiritual war...whether you decide you *want* to be in it or not. It doesn't matter whether you *choose* to defend yourself against the enemy or not. You may say, "I don't know what you're talking about. I'm doing just fine." Well, there is a saying that if Satan is not bothering you, it may be because you're holding hands with him! The Bible warns us to put on the *whole armor* of God.

Satan uses many devices to accomplish his mission of destruction. He attacks those who are either the biggest threat or the biggest potential threat. He tried to kill the baby Jesus because He saw what might be coming in the future.

Often, his strategy is to be invisible. (Like the stalker that tried to hurt Cheryl.) We think that we are experiencing human, physical problems when all the time Satan is orchestrating the problems.

Satan is *"the accuser of the brethren."* (Revelations 10:12) He will tell you that "it's all your fault, you are the only one who has problems like this...or my personal favorite...this situation will never change it will always be this bad." We must not be ignorant of the devices of Satan! When we know what the enemy is up to, we can fight him.

One of the big devices he uses is to fasten a curse to you and your family. A spirit attaches itself to one of your ancestors and finds a home in your family. It is comfortable there. This curse or spirit is able to come in because we are caught unaware...or because our ancestors let the devil come into their lives.

When we marry a non-Christian...or we become friends with a person who doesn't love the Lord...this allows Satan to have a foothold in our lives. *A foothold is all Satan needs to eventually build a stronghold!* He may stay in our family tree for generations. There is no such thing as harmless casual relationships with people who don't love the Lord. If you marry an unbeliever, they can have a negative impact on your life and the lives of your children. If you are friends with nonbelievers, they can be contagious. You may love the person but be aware that his influence could cause you to turn away from the Lord.

If you are already married to an unbeliever, the Word of God has already taken care of it. I Corinthians 7:14 (Amplified) "For the unbelieving husband is set apart (separated, withdrawn from heathen contamination, and affiliated with the Christian people) by union with his consecrated (set-apart) wife, and the unbelieving wife is set apart and separated through union with the consecrated husband. Otherwise your children would be unclean (unblessed heathen, outside the Christian covenant), but as it is they are *prepared* for God good and clean."

I Peter 3:1 says "In like manner, you married women, be submissive to your own husbands (subordinate yourselves as being secondary to and dependent on them, and adapt yourselves to them), so that even if any do not obey the Word (of God), they may be won over not by discussion but by the (godly) lives of their wives. When they observe the pure and modest way in which you conduct yourselves, together with your reverence (for your husband; you are to feel for him all that reverence includes: to respect, defer to, revere him—to honor, esteem, appreciate, prize, and, in the human sense to adore him, that is to admire, praise, be devoted to, deeply love and enjoy your husband)."

But these verses don't mean that it's going to be easy. You have a spiritual fight on your hands so...keep your armor on!

Where the anointing abounds, Satan is lurking around. If you are a Christian, Satan is just waiting for the proper opportunity to take you out. You are a target being stalked by Satan. A stalker is quiet and is secretly scouring the area looking for a way to gain entrance. He is like a rat in a wall...sneaking in and out without being noticed. He's waiting for you to slip, to entertain something from his world so he can slip in.

If your family has allowed this spirit to come in, you must take action...and cast the spirit out of your family in the Name of Jesus.

Ephesians 4:27 counsels us not to "give *place* to the devil." Part of not giving place is *"living consciously"* knowing what is going on around us. Being watchful. (Police say that criminals watch for people who are unaware of what is going on around them because they are easy prey.) Understand that your actions will bless you or curse you. All actions have consequences...good or bad. If you do not cast the demonic spirit out, it will invite other spirits to come and live with it. Even good people...Christians...can have an evil spirit attach to themselves and their families. When you see a string of disastrous and destructive events begin to happen in a family, these events should be suspect to enemy attack.

If a curse has come into your family you must bind Satan in the Name of Jesus. *"When you resist the devil he must flee!"* (James 4:7) Run Satan out of your life...and the lives of your family. The good news is that you can break the generation to generation curse. You can take authority over it, bind it and cast it out of your life and the lives of your offspring. You can break the cycle.

Most of us don't realize it but the supernatural evil world is physically close to the supernatural good world. The worlds are not that far away from each other...with the flip of a switch...your vote of yes or no...you can enter either world. The choice is always yours. Choose life and faith!

Deuteronomy 30:19 (Amplified) "I call heaven and earth to witness this day against you that I have set before you life and death, the blessings and the curses; therefore choose life, that you and your descendents may live."

When *faith* enters a family tree it also impacts generations to come. Faith definitely passes from generation to generation. Often unsaved adults, who are now seeking the Lord, tell of a Christian grandparent or other relative that had an influence on their lives. God is faithful to those Saints who stood in the gap for their families. Parents with unsaved children claim the promise, *"Train up a child in the way he should go (and in keeping with his individual gift or bent), and when he is old he will not depart from it."* (Proverbs 22:6, Amplified) God honors the faith of those parents.

Generational blessings belong to us as Christians. Many of us do not know our spiritual roots. We are unaware of the blessings of family heritage that are ours.

Think about the blessings we have simply because we are Americans. Today, America receives the blessings of God because our forefathers came here to establish their religious freedom. They didn't come here for wealth or because they were greedy. They just wanted to worship in freedom. God has blessed our country because of these early roots. Today, believers and nonbelievers alike enjoy these blessings. God continues to bless our country because of the large number of believers who live here. Nonbelievers benefit from the overflow of these blessings of God.

The blessings of God are "kept in the family" and

passed from generation to generation. God told Abraham that *"I will bless those who bless you and curse those who curse you; and the entire world will be blessed because of you. ...I am going to give this land to your descendents."* (Genesis 12:3,7, Living Bible) There are many instances in the Bible where people even reminded God that He promised to bless them. It is OK to remind God, "I am living my life in a righteous manner (the best way I know how). I claim Your blessings on my life and the lives of my family. I am living expectantly. I am resting and trusting You, Father, that You will bring health and prosperity to me and my loved ones."

"My rest and trust is not passive...it is active because I can't wait to see what you will do for me and my family. Just as you opened the Red Sea for the children of Israel so they could pass...You have worked many miracles in my life and the lives of my family and I can't wait to see the blessings and miracles You will bestow on us today! I can't wait to see the character and spirituality you will help me develop!"

God promised the Israelites many blessings but He didn't just hand the blessings over to them. There were giants living in the *land flowing with milk and honey.* They had to *"claim"* their blessings and take the land. Today, God has given us many blessings but it is necessary for us to discover what those blessings are by reading our Bible. *We must claim our blessings and run Satan off our property.*

Many men do not know that there is a spiritual war taking place for their souls. They are not aware that Satan is trying to steal their blessings.

We have a picture of Satan as some cartoon character not to be taken seriously. This is not what the Bible tells us. Who is Satan? In Isaiah 14:12 it says, *"How art thou fallen from heaven, O Lucifer, son of the morning! How art thou cut down to the ground, which did weaken the nations! For thou hast said in thine heart, I will ascend into heaven, I will exalt my throne above the stars of God: I will sit also upon the mount of the congregation, in the sides of the north: (in the place of control) I will ascend above the heights of the clouds; I will be like the most High. Yet thou shall be brought down to hell."*

Not only did Satan think he was equal to God but he was jealous of God. In his mind, he could not stand for there to be another like himself. Because of his jealousy of God's Son he wanted to take Jesus out while He was on this earth. He wanted to stop Him before He had a chance to complete the task God sent Him to do...to save mankind.

Satan stalked Jesus. His main objective was to kill Him. Satan tried to deceive Jesus into believing that he had the power to offer Jesus the world. (Satan has deceived many into believing that he could offer the riches of the world to them.) Matthew 4 tells us that Jesus went into the wilderness and was tempted by Satan. Each time Satan tried to tempt Him, Jesus answered, *"It is written..."* He used the Word to fight Satan and win!

Satan finally realized he couldn't win with this approach so he used ordinary people to attack Jesus. Eventually these people killed Him. Satan thought he had won. But he had made a terrible mistake. He did not know that Jesus' death saved people from their sins. Satan had been set up! Sunday was coming...when Jesus rose from the grave. Satan thought he had been victorious in the death of Jesus. On Sunday morning, when the tomb was empty he realized that God had won the battle! This angered Satan and that is why today he is stalking our families with a vengeance. This is why he is trying to steal the things that God has given to you.

Today, Satan is stalking the families of God with a vengeance. Most of the time you are unaware of the negative activities taking place around you. Satan is behind many of our negative thoughts. He tries to make you feel angry, or envious, or guilty. The Bible calls these "works of the flesh" in Galatians 5. Satan uses our flesh against us. That's why we must keep our flesh "down" and our spirits built up! He is also behind many of the negative attacks on you. Many of his attacks are military in nature. If one attack doesn't work he'll try another.

Never forget that we are on the winning side! You can win over the devil. God has given you all the necessary tools. We need to do several things to protect ourselves. 1) You must know Jesus Christ as your Personal Savior. 2) You need to have a regular program for reading your Bible. 3) You should pray a special prayer covering over yourself and your loved ones. 4) Be aware that demons may have attached themselves to your forefathers. You must clean them out by rebuking them and breaking the generational curse in the Name of Jesus. 5) You must also claim and expect your blessings from God.

I John 4:4 "Greater is He (God) Who is in us than he that is in the world." Satan is in the world, not *in* us. Scripture says God is the Great I Am. The Great I Am is in us, and we have His authority to use his name. We can resist the devil when he attacks us. We are not a second class people...because God is not a second class God. Satan is the loser, the counterfeit, and the one in danger. Satan knows it but only when we take our proper authority in breaking curses off our family will he leave. (James 4:7)

Repeat after me, *"Satan, in the Powerful Name of Jesus I rebuke you...I bind you from having any power over my life or the lives of my family. The Bible says that when I resist you, you must flee.* Therefore, in the mighty name of Jesus of Nazareth I continually and constantly resist you and you must flee now in Jesus name!"

— CHAPTER EIGHT —

INTIMACY...INTO ME SEE!

What is the first thing you think about when someone talks about being intimate? Sex, right? That's because our whole society focuses on sex. The gyms are full of people trying to attract mates with their beautiful bodies. Don't get me wrong...a good physical appearance is important. Unfortunately, there are thousands of people who are beautiful on the outside but miserable on the inside.

This may surprise you but an attractive physical appearance cannot bring happiness to you in and of itself. Many a man has grown tired of his "beautiful" bride when he discovers that she has no character.

OK. Let's talk about beauty and sex. People who subscribe to the "appearance and sex" group spend much more time focusing on the outside than on the inside. Often they don't value health of the spirit and character. Again this is not to say that we shouldn't be healthy or fit. It is only when there is an obsession with the outer appearance, to the exclusion of inner qualities, that there are problems.

You cannot assume that when you have a beautiful wife you will be able to establish an emotionally intimate relationship with her. As we'll discuss later, it takes love and effort to have a strong, intimate relationship.

So when I talk about intimacy...I'm not necessarily

talking about sex. In fact, true intimacy has nothing to do with physical contact... although when you take the time and care to develop an intimate personal relationship with your wife it will enhance your sexual relationship as well.

Many people, who do not have emotionally intimate relationships walk through life like zombies. They are unhappy and unfulfilled. This is definitely not what God intended! He wanted husbands and wives to enjoy each other.

Remember, when you first started dating your wife? Your head was full of thoughts about her. You couldn't wait to see her...and you couldn't wait to talk with her. Then you got married and through the years you started taking each other for granted. There were differences that started piling up inside you. Many of these differences you held inside you. You never expressed to her how hurt you felt over something she said or did. You threw those things into your *"emotional trashcan."* Year after year things piled up. One therapist said it well. *"It's like keeping a dead body in the basement...after a while it starts to stink!"* Old unresolved garbage is one of the main reasons that couples just *"Go through the motions of life."*

Remember when you first made love to your wife? It didn't matter that you were exhausted from work or that you had a lot of business matters on your mind. Your thoughts and love for your mate made you want to be one with her. God meant for the love of a man and wife to be a physical, emotional and spiritual experience. This was God's plan not man's. When your heart is full of the ways you love your wife you will want to express that love to her.

You may ask, "What am I supposed to do so my wife

73

and I can become emotionally intimate with each other?" One of the most important things you can do is establish ground rules. *Agree from this point that you will conduct your relationship in a positive way.*

1) When an issue is important to one person in the partnership it should be important to both. There are some things that are a "1" in your mind. Your wife may consider the same issue to be a "10." Problems occur when the partner who sees it as a "1" ignores, belittles, or ridicules their mate's perspective. It is better to say, "Whoops. Was that a "10" for you?" You can even laugh together over your differences. Knowing that you acknowledge the difference helps a lot. Then sit down and let the other person unload how they feel. You will become much closer and you won't drive important feelings underground. Feelings driven underground will cause problems when they *pop up* unexpectedly.

2) Agree *never* to say negative things to each other. Agree not to criticize, condemn, or complain. When you are critical of your wife, she will start to close up...like a beautiful flower. When that flower closes it is hard to get it to open up again. Develop good communication skills that will help you tell the other person when something is bothering you. We should always remember that when we communicate to our partner that they have dignity and worth, then they will act like *they* have dignity and worth. This perspective says, "I won't just try to drive my point home...I'll remember that she is a valuable person and has her own perspective." It's hard to shout at someone or degrade them when you keep these things in mind.

3) Agree not to use *hurtful humor* to get your point

74

across. Many couples say very hurtful things to their partners and laugh about it as though it were a joke. This is anger in disguise. If we have emptied our emotional trashcans in a healthy way, we won't have any ammunition left to use. We also won't have the desire to lash out. We use the *teapot method* and just let a little bit of our displeasure come out at a time. Don't disguise your anger in humor or be critical. When you have to address an employee at work over some grievance, you talk in a positive way about the problem. You don't run the employee into the ground. You know that if you handle the situation that way you will have a very unhappy employee...or an absent employee.

4) Learn to validate your wife's feelings. What does that mean? Man by his very nature wants to fix things and solve problems. I'm no exception. Women many times do not want to have their problems solved...they just want to talk about them. When your wife tells you about a problem, don't swing into action and give her a solution. Validate her feelings by saying, "That must have made you angry or I know you must really be frustrated about that or I'll bet you were frightened or how in the world could that person do that to you, etc." *She will let you know when she needs the problem solved.*

5) Learn good communication skills. Don't just talk for the sake of talking, really communicate. Eliminate words like *"you always, you never."* This takes your conversation out of the present and off the point you were discussing. Don't attack your partner by ordering your wife "You do this...." Communication is not a verbal behavior. "Having just the right words" is not as important as "How you express your message." Don't use explosive words...they enrage people. The medical community gives us a good example. "You

might feel a slight discomfort with this..." When you need to tell your partner about feelings say, "When this happens, I feel lonely. I feel fearful that I'm not important to you anymore." It pays big dividends to make yourself vulnerable to each other. It is difficult to be angry with a person when they have made themselves vulnerable to you. Instead it makes the other person feel very intimate and close to you.

6) When your wife makes herself vulnerable to you, or vice versa, you must agree never to use this information in a negative way...even in joking. If you do not honor your wife's vulnerability she will close up and put her anger and hurt feelings in her *emotional trashcan*. When this happens her feelings will *"numb"* toward you. There won't be any fights on the surface but she will push those feelings down and when this happens the good feelings go underground with the bad ones. If you are feeling numb it's probably because you have pushed negative feelings down, too.

Also, childhood pain can be stuffed into the trashcan. Adult children of workaholics, alcoholics, and abusers should bring up those old feelings and deal with them. Adult children are often hesitant to do this because they say that if they ever start crying they won't stop. You may cry at first but these feelings will pass. This is part of the grief process you are going through from the past. You go through all the stages with this process—denial, anger, pain, acceptance. Having the courage to go through the process can bring much healing. Many times we need to have funerals for the past. We need to grieve, cry and then bury the ghost of the past so we can have a healthy present and future.

7) Agree not to use nonverbal behavior to commu-

nicate your displeasure. Don't slam doors, throw pots and pans around, give the silent treatment, refuse to listen to each other, heave big sighs, refuse to look at the other person, refuse to stay in the same room. The list goes on and on. What you are saying is, "I'm angry but I'm not going to trust you to talk about it." Many times the mate can only guess why you are angry. When they have to guess what's wrong most of the time they come to the wrong conclusion. Then they get upset, too. It is always better to talk as long as you don't use words that attack, undermine or belittle. These situations can actually draw you closer to each other.

8) Think about planning a "date night" with your wife. It can be as simple as staying home and turning off the TV, taking the children to the sitter or grand-parents, turning on romantic music and lighting a room full of candles. Agree to talk about things like "how you felt the first time you met."

Learn to become *one* with your wife. The Bible says that when you are joined together you become one flesh. Your wife needs to be your intimate partner and friend. She needs to feel that she is attractive to you. She needs to feel close to you. You need to feel close to someone, too. Love your wife as you love yourself. When you love your wife you *are* loving yourself. Treat your wife the way you would like her to treat you. Let me ask you, "If you aren't the person to love your wife, who is?"

True intimacy is "into me see," as Cheryl says. See into each other's heart. Open up and talk and share with each other. If you have both agreed to the ground rules it's safe to talk to each other. (It is extremely important not to violate these ground rules.) You will feel as if a load has been lifted off your shoulders when you talk. There is no greater trust than to allow some-one "in" to your life, nothing between you—no clothes, no covers, no walls—just you and me. That's true trust—no fear of rejection.

Do things for your wife. I'm not necessarily talking about some big, expensive gift. Bring home an inex-pensive bouquet of flowers and surprise her at the door. One husband noticed that his wife's shoes needed pol-ished. He asked, "Are you going to wear these today?" When he found out that she planned to wear them that day, he picked them up and polished them only minutes before he left for work. A little thing? In a marriage, the little things *are* the big things!

Give your wife your time and attention. There has been a lot of literature written talking about spending "quality time" with your loved ones but the fact of the matter is that it will never replace quantity time! If your work load is too heavy to allow time with your wife and children, you may want to consider changing it. Your "work" is a vehicle to care for your family. Work should not consume all of our time. Many a workaholic husband didn't wake up and smell the coffee until their wife filed for divorce and it was too late!

Don't take your wife or what she does for granted. Notice when she has prepared a good meal or done something special to the house. Tell her when you are proud of her. Tell her she is beautiful as you did when you first met. Tell others in her presence how proud you are of her. Mark Twain said, "A good compliment will last me a good two weeks." Don't forget to say thank you.

Good listening is the key to an intimate relationship. You always learn much more when you listen. (You've already heard everything you know.) So listen to your wife. Turn off the television. I say turn off the television because most men are like I was. They get caught up in sports on television. Does this sound like you? "OK, talk the commercial is on. OK, stop the commercial is over and the game is back on."

Your wife is more important than the game on television but we won't interrupt our game to listen to something important she has to tell us. We don't treat her like what she has to say is important. Here's a good test to see if you are truly intimate with your wife. Hand her the remote control to the television when you are both in the room. If you can trust your wife with the remote control you can trust yourself to become intimate with her. Sound stupid? Ask your wife when was the last time you gave her the remote control button. Then ask her when was the last time you had an intimate or private conversation. The conversation you had in the bedroom doesn't count. That conversation is important but not at this time.

If she shows surprise that you're asking...you have your answer. If she looks at you and says, "You want me to have the remote? Me?" Then you have your answer. Without realizing it we have lost that intimate time with our wives...and probably with our family and even God. I'll bet you hold the remote control more in one day than you hold your wife's hand in a week!

I Peter 3:7 (Amplified) says, "In the same manner you married men should live considerately with (your wives), with an intelligent recognition (of the marriage relationship), honoring the woman as (physically) the weaker, but (realizing that you are joint heirs of the grace (God's unmerited favor) of life, in order that your prayers may not be hindered and cut off. (Otherwise you cannot pray effectively.)"

God does not treat the care we give our wives lightly. He tells us that when we don't treat our wives well it will hinder our prayer life!

It's equally important to be intimate with your children. In a recent article I read that most men spend only three minutes of quality time a week with their children. Three minutes. That time that we could have spent with our families is lost forever.

We spend more time watching television or driving to work than three minutes a week. We have to ask ourselves, "How can my children trust me if they have no time to get to know me and be intimate with me?" I don't give them enough time for them to tell me what is bothering them or what is hurting them. They have no time to let down their walls and communicate with me. Our children need good friends but more importantly they need good parents...parents who will spend time with them. Again, don't be fooled by the old idea that quality time is more important than quantity time. Our children need both quality and quantity time. Make the quantity time, quality time.

Take time to listen, play, and work with your children. Live life to the fullest with them. Don't be in such a hurry to get ahead in life that you don't enjoy the experience of life itself...good, bad, or indifferent. You know, it's not your vacation destination that is exciting, it's who is going on the vacation. It's not exciting if you arrive on vacation alone. What is important is that you are sharing your vacation with your loved ones...that you're building happy memories with them. When you are old and sitting in your rocking chair at the end of your life, you will cherish those great memories of spending time with your wife and children. (Ps. 22:30, Eph. 1:11)

It pleases God when we make special efforts to show our loved ones how much we care. These actions make strong families that can serve the Lord.

— CHAPTER NINE —

AN INTIMATE RELATIONSHIP WITH GOD

It is important that we have an intimate relationship with God. This is where most men get scared off. It isn't in our character to be intimate with God. God is in the sky and we are down here. We throw our prayers up to God in heaven from a distance and that is OK with us. We are comfortable with that. Many of us think that God is like our earthly father. If you had a strong relationship with your father, that's great. If your father was distant to you or absent from the home a lot or menacing in his attitude toward you, you can have a few bad memories. We have to learn to trust God and know like   Deuteronomy 31:6 says *"He will never leave us or forsake us."*

There are men's groups that help bridge the gap between men and God. Demos Shakarian, founder of Full Gospel Businessmen was one of the first men to see that there are more women than men attending church. It was his dream to mobilize men to have a deeper walk with God. In his book *The Happiest People on Earth* , Demos told Oral Roberts about his dream. The year was 1951. "It's a group of men. Not exceptional men. Just average business people who know the Lord and love Him but haven't known how to show it. They tell other men, Oral. No theories. They tell what they've actually experienced of God to other men like themselves—men who might not believe what a preacher said—even someone like you—but who will listen to a plumber or a dentist or a salesman because they're plumbers and dentists and salesmen themselves. Whatever the man's experience, he could talk about it, just as it happened." For over 40 years, this group has been instrumental in helping men all over the world develop a deeper walk with God.

In 1990, University of Colorado Football Coach, Bill McCartney founded Promise Keepers, an International Christian Group just for men. By 1995, more than 700,000 men had attended inspirational rallies staged at 13 stadiums around the country. Promise Keepers promotes male leadership in the home and a closer walk with God. Thousands of men all over the world attend their rallies held in huge stadiums. Many of these functions sell out months ahead of time.

I mention these groups because they are an excellent way to develop a deeper walk with God. But it goes further than this, you have to get alone with God, long after the meetings are over. Spend private time with God.

God is moving greatly in the lives of men. Men are unashamedly confessing their relationship with God. In a recent article, called *Playing by God's Rules by George Diaz* that appeared in the Orlando Sentinal, athletes unashamedly professed their close personal relationship with God.

"Heavyweight Champion, Evander Holyfield, became an inspirational beacon after he was cast as a 25-1 underdog against a menacing, street-tough champion whose most recent challengers had crumbled in pain. Skeptics assumed Holyfield would be next.

"Holyfield, sweat trickling down his bald head, gave a quizzical expression to one of those skeptics who asked what he expected to see when he faced "Iron" Mike Tyson.

"A victory, my hand raised and giving all the praise and glory to the Lord," Holyfield said. "I'm no different from the next man. I hurt, too, when I get hit. Sometimes fear jumps up in my heart, but you have to have something to cast that fear out to take a step to go forward. I came from a praying family. They always prayed for me, and I learned to pray for myself, which is more important. I can't live without prayer in every phase of my life."

"Walking into the ring wearing purple robes inscribed with "Philippians 4:13 ("I have strength for all things in Christ Who empowers me (I am ready for anything and equal to anything through Him Who infuses inner strength into me; I am self-sufficient in Christ's sufficiency.) Holy field scored an 11th round technical knockout, a victory some observers noted *had* to be rigged with divine intervention.

"Reflecting his strong religious roots, Holyfield gathers his trainers, sparring partners, and others in his camp before every training session for a prayer. They form a circle and clasp hands.

"Thank you, Lord, for being here and watching over us, and thank you for keeping us as one," a voice within the circle said recently. "And thank you for watching over and continuing to watch over 'Holy.'"

Once the training begins, Holyfield pumps loud gospel tunes from a CD boom box positioned nest to the ring.

"The first thing Evander and I did before we ever broke a sweat together was pray," said Tim Hallmark, a conditioning guru who has been with Holyfield for more than a decade. "I truly believe to this day, that was the foundation that made our friendship so strong. What's made both of our lives so powerful is not only our religion but our relationship with Jesus Christ. That's the one thing we both have in common. If we had nothing else in common except that one thing, that was enough to develop a very strong relationship.

"In 1996, University of Florida's Football Player Danny Wuerffel won the Heisman Trophy and immediately acknowledged his religious convictions during his acceptance speech: "I just want to give all the glory and praise to God. He is the rock upon which I stand. Publicly, I'd like to ask Him to forgive me of my sins for they are many." Wuerffel continues to praise a higher power for his success. Images of Wuerffel clasping his hands in prayer after every touchdown were prominent in weekly highlight films.

"Coming from a family with a rich religious heritage of ministers on both sides, Wuerffel naturally embraced his Lutheran-based Christian convictions. Using his position as president of the University of Florida chapter of the FCA, Wuerffel has used his fame as a platform to spread the Word. Consider this sound bite from New York earlier this month, when Wuerffel accepted the Heisman: "It's a blessing to be here. It's a blessing to play college football, but the biggest blessing of all is I'm so thankful that nothing could compare to the knowledge of knowing and having and living relationship with Jesus.

"Using another medium, Wuerffel wrote an essay in *Sports Spectrum Magazine,* a religious publication, on his celebratory habit after touchdowns.

"As a Christian athlete—a Christian who happens to

be an athlete, and not vice versa—I have found that folding my hands together following each touchdown is a humble way of thanking the Lord for the gifts and opportunities He has so graciously bestowed upon me," Wuerffel wrote. "Praying wasn't anything I planned or decided to do, but I found it to be as natural as spotting an open receiver and instinctively throwing the ball. A touchdown is a natural point of closure—-a perfect occasion to humble express gratitude to the One who gave me the gifts and the opportunity to use them; the author of Hebrews calls this *the sacrifice of praise.*"

Men, it's time for us to get out of our comfort zone. Wouldn't you like to have a relationship with God like these athletes? You can. God is in you...right next to you. If you are a Christian, Jesus is even closer...He is in you. My little girl, Gabrielle, shared her perspective of Jesus with me.

"Daddy, I can't see Jesus. Do you know why?"

"No," I said.

"Because He is in my heart and I can't see in there. I wish I could see him."

"I know but you can *feel* Him. Just put your hand over your heart and feel your heart beat." I assured her.

"Yes, I can," she said with a twinkle in her eye.

Anytime you want to know that Jesus is near, just put your hand over your heart and close your eyes. You can feel Him in each beat of your heart. He is right there making your heart beat.

God wants to be intimate with you. He wants to be so close that He is actually inside you. Share your time with God and He will share His desires *for* you...and *with* you.

I had to experience a crisis in my life for me to see that God wants me to have an intimate relationship with Him...not a long distance one. Sometimes families try to work out a long distance relationship, where a father lives in one state and the mother and the children in another. These families have found out through hard experiences that long distance relationships just don't work. Eventually the man and woman grow apart. It won't work for man...and it definitely won't work with God.

It's not God's way to move away from you. However, you will grow away from Him if you don't spend time with Him. I know this from experience.

I have worked for the Oral Roberts Association for over 17 years. I have served the ministry in the area of television and management all these years. I have been around faith people...I have listened to hundreds of testimonies but it wasn't until my wife Cheryl became sick with depression that I felt the need to get close and intimate with God.

I had always gone to church but much of the spiritual leadership I left to my wife Cheryl, who is a minister. When she was unable to function in this role it was up to me to pray with the children and to believe God for Cheryl's healing. When this happened it was a real wake up call. I began to read my Bible more and pray and really get close to God. I can just tell you that it has been a great experience...even though it was hard for me in many ways. I would *never* go back to the long distance relationship I had with God.

It's so simple. Just sit down and begin to tell God how you feel.

Pull down the walls of protection you have built

around yourself. Trust God. Let those walls come down. Let down those defenses. The walls you have built around yourself separate you from people. A wall is an obstruction between things that *need* to blend together.

Once you begin to talk with God intimately and really communicate with Him, He will begin to talk to you and reveal things to you. This is how it works. You will receive impressions in your mind and heart. At first you will think it is your own mind. But when you read your Bible and begin to know and understand Christian principles, you will know when it is Him. John 10:27 says, *"My sheep will recognize my voice."* Your communication becomes a two way relationship. You ask questions and then you receive answers from God. You give of yourself and your time and He gives back to you the desires of your heart.

Each time God works miracles in your life your faith grows stronger. (You might want to keep a **miracle journal** to remind you of the things that God has done for you...it can be a real faith builder.) God tells us the secret of having a rich, happy life. He gives us guidance on the things that will give us true happiness, joy and peace. God has coded the secrets. You will not understand the secrets unless you become hungry to be close to God. When you come close to God you learn to trust Him. God gives us the most powerful revelations when we commit to spend time with Him. Men who are casually interested in God do not receive the same revelations that committed men of faith receive. Hebrews 11:6 says, *"But without faith it is impossible to please and be satisfactory to Him. For whoever would come near to God must believe that God exists and that He is the **Rewarder** of those who earnestly and diligently* *seek Him.*"

Earnestly and diligently. When you earnestly seek God, you are sincerely seeking Him with your heart, heart felt. When you diligently seek God, you seek Him without ceasing. Make it a heartfelt relationship that will not let anything stop it or stand in your way.

I Corinthians 6:17 says, *"But anyone united with the Lord becomes one spirit with Him."* Remember you are one with God. You are a King's Kid. Don't take that for granted...spend time with Him because He wants to spend time with you. He wants to bless you.

— CHAPTER TEN —

A HERITAGE OF "BEING TOUGH!"

"Don't be a sucker for anybody." Those were the last words my dad ever spoke to me. In my mind, if I fell short of his direction, I was a failure. Even as a young boy, I felt tremendous pressure on me to be successful and tough. I had to be a man, no matter what. My father told me not to show my feelings. He told me I should never talk about my feelings. He said that if I let anybody know how I felt it was a sign of weakness. It was not good to let anyone get close to me.

I found out that there are big problems when you seal yourself in behind *protective walls*. You may be protected from some pain but there are many things you are unable to experience.

1) *You do not trust anyone*. Your distrust makes you suspicious. You are always wondering about people's motives. Do they want to do you harm? That same feeling is transferred to your relationship with God. Your relationship with God is not built upon trust...because you do not trust anybody. You may feel suspicious, untrusting and unwilling to come too close to God for fear of being hurt. He might ask you to do something that you don't want to do.

You don't confess many of your sins because even God shouldn't know too much about you. He might use it against you.

One of the most valuable, satisfying things you can ever experience in your life is a personal relationship with God. At any hour of the day or night you can talk to your Friend. You can tell Him your hopes and your dreams. You can lay your pain and depression at His feet. You can ask Him to help you not to want to live in the flesh. Living in this world, not God's world, causes pain. When we operate in the flesh, we are "living in hate, greed, selfishness, and anger." I don't know about you but I don't want to live in toxic waste like that! I would much rather live in hope, love, joy, peace, and rest...the things that are opposite of living in the flesh.

2) *Being "tough" can cause problems in your relationship with your wife.* You must make yourself vulnerable to your wife in order for you to have a good relationship with her. You have to share your feelings. If you don't open up and let your mate, for instance, know what you are thinking...they have to guess what your thoughts and actions mean. Often they guess wrong. Frustration, bitterness and even hate can begin to build up inside them. There is an underlying hostility that develops all because of being unable to let down those walls and trust her and communicate with her.

3) "Tough guys" have health problems. When you bottle up your emotions they impact the immune system, blood and internal organs. There is a saying that *"You bury your feelings alive."* If you doubt this think about some situation that was traumatic in your life. It may have been years since it happened but the tears still come when you remember it. You should talk about your feelings and get them out of your system. I don't think you need to wallow in your problems continuously but you do need to let them see the light of day.

You need to go through the stages of grief with pain. I did not do this. I let the pressures of being responsible for the management of the ministry weigh heavy on my mind and body. I finally collapsed with chest pains. The Bible says in I Peter 2:9 "...called you out of darkness into this marvelous light." Get it out into God's light!

4) *Walls can lead to addiction.* Some people use drugs, alcohol, gambling. Many are co-dependent. They deny that they have needs of their own. In my case I often used food that was not good for me to numb the frustration I felt. I loved to eat pizza and foods that were high in fat. When I did that it added to the stress my body was already experiencing. My cholesterol was over 500. Take my word for it... walls can damage your health.

5) *Walls keep you from feeling the juice of life!* Therapists say that when you keep the walls up and don't allow full disclosure, you can *numb out.* You will find that you just don't feel anything...good or bad. You may think it's stress from work when it's unresolved feelings. Evidently, when you stuff painful issues, and hold them on the inside of you, the good emotions are stuffed on the inside of you too. If you want to be joyful...clean out your emotional trashcan.

I can still remember my wife, Cheryl, asking me if I would please smile in our family pictures. I didn't smile much. I said, "I *am* smiling." In my mind I was smiling! Then I remembered my dad telling me, "Don't you smile in any pictures." I didn't know what he meant. Don't ever let yourself get in that state. I now know that he was saying, "Don't smile and show your teeth that are missing." I was eight years old with no front teeth but I misunderstood what he said to me as a little boy. It took years until my mother finally explained it to me.

My mother reared me by herself and did the best she could to instill openness and sensitivity in me. It was difficult as a man to incorporate her teaching into my life because the shadow of my powerful father fell over my life! It raised a lot of conflict in me. I received her teaching regarding good manners and other things. But I questioned being open. It was contrary to what my father told me to do or so I thought.

A son looks up to his father...even if he is giving him information that is in error and can cause him pain. It takes a lot of years to break down those walls. Unfortunately, many men are never able to get over their upbringing. It is only through the powerful love of Jesus Christ that the pain from the past is healed.

I thought I had to be the toughest man alive. I could never let my emotions get the best of me. I could never let my guard down. Above all I should never let anyone or anybody know I hurt or that I was in trouble. I had to keep my problems to myself. My identity as a man was at stake. My heritage as a strong middle eastern man was at stake. I was the son of a man who told me never to be weak or in his words *"a sucker."* My heritage was to be tough.

My "tough" code of behavior was not just for people...it was for God, too! Deep down I knew that God knew everything I felt, did or was going through but I still resisted Him. God was up in heaven and I consented to let Him take care of me from a distance. I thought it would be a personal imposition to call on Him for a personal need of mine. I was a strong man...I could handle the situation no matter what. Besides, in my mind, God had so many other needy people to help...starving children, and people with terminal illnesses.

It wasn't until I experienced a crisis in my life that I began to discover my true identity and heritage. My wife, Cheryl, had a miscarriage. We lost our precious baby. It hit me particularly hard because Cheryl and I have a very special love for our children. We really *value* our children. When this happened I was in pain but I couldn't grieve over the loss. Then I had to explain the miscarriage to Lil' Harry. He asked me, "What did we name the baby we had lost?" He said, "We need to name him because we need to know what to call him. When we get to heaven we can call him by name."

His words hit me hard. It helped me begin to feel the pain of the loss. I started thinking about my loss. Naming the fetus brought closure to the loss of my child. It was my child too and I hurt deep inside. I learned it was OK to grieve for that loss. I released my feelings and was able to cry for the first time. You see my dad always told me, "It is a sign of weakness in a man to cry." He told me not to cry at his funeral because I had to be strong for the family. He told me I had to be the head of the family. I was 10 years old.

It was through my son that the little boy inside me allowed himself to have emotions and feelings. In that moment my son helped me draw close to *Jesus in a very personal way. Jesus became the personal Lord of my life through that experience.* Don't get me wrong. Jesus was my Savior but He wasn't the Lord of my life. I hadn't let Him be the Lord of my life because I would not let down the protective walls or guard I had built around myself. These walls prevented me from letting Him come into my heart in a personal way.

I had let just enough of Him in to call Him my Savior...but not enough to let Him be my leader. I hadn't let Him be my best friend or Father, a motivating force in my life. I discovered that I had received my *true heritage* when my Savior died for me two thousand years ago...not when I was a little boy. My inheritance is the Kingdom of Heaven not a car dealership in Michigan. My true identity is that of husband, daddy, and servant...not some false person with walls higher than the Empire State Building. I am a man with feelings and I can share them with others and not be less of a man.

Many of you have had similar experiences in your life. All your life your father taught you to be tough. Well, this is a lie from the devil. You don't have to be tough anymore. True strength comes from God. You don't have to be emasculated to have a Father-son relationship with God, you just have to be a son.

— CHAPTER ELEVEN —

"DO WHAT IT TAKES...NOT JUST WHAT YOU CAN!"

There is a statement that I heard when I was a little boy that I have remembered all of my life. "Do what it takes...not what you can."

When someone asks you to do something for them, you might answer, "Well, I'll see what I can do...or I will do what I can."

When Cheryl became sick and eventually went through many, many months of depression, I asked myself "What can I do?" The depression lasted for eighteen months. My initial thought was, "I'll do what I can...I'll look into it." Then it struck me. *"You can't just do what you can. You have to do what it takes!"* I knew if the roles were reversed Cheryl would have not just stopped at doing what she could do. She would have gone much, much further. She would do whatever it took.

The fact that I'm a man made me do everything in my power to "fix something," fix her illness. I was doing all I could stop the problem. Physical problems were what I knew how to fix.

For instance, if my little boy broke a toy he would bring it to me to fix. I could usually fix it because it was something physical that I could manipulate. This works fine when you are dealing with simple, physical things.

What happens when we need something fixed that is out of our control? Cheryl's depression was eventually "fixed" through prayer and medication but we first had to get a grip on what was happening to her. We had to use all of our resources to get it fixed.

I knew that I had to tap into that Source that Cheryl had when she was a little girl in Choctaw County, Mississippi. She went to the hospital after her car accident. She lay there in excruciating pain with a crushed leg. All her doctors, friends and even church people tried to make her accept the fact that she would be crippled for the rest of her life. Cheryl refused to listen to them.

Cheryl did what it took! She addressed the supernatural and got out of the natural. She expanded her beliefs. She looked past those things that are seen and focused on the unseen. *If we believe more in those things we cannot see—the supernatural—than we do in the things we can see—in the natural we will have what we cannot see.* Cheryl believed in what she couldn't see. She saw her leg whole and healed. She saw herself not as a cripple but as a miracle.

My mother was a young woman when my father died. If she had listened to all the people around her—even her minister—she would probably have split the family up. She refused to accept the fact that it would be better to split up three young children and take them away from their mother. My mother did not stop at doing what she could, *she did what it took!*

Determined to do the best for her children, she poured over scripture seeking God's guidance. She found a scripture that gave her comfort through the tough times. *"I will be the Father to the widows and* orphans." (Psalm 146:9) She did not look at her circumstances in the natural...she put her trust and belief in the supernatural. Daily, she put her belief into action while she raised three young children by herself. She did what it took to keep her family together and see all her grandchildren born.

There is story of a little boy who was afraid to sleep alone in his room at night. His daddy said, "Jesus is always there with you. You don't need to be afraid." The little boy said in an innocent voice, "I know that daddy but I just need someone with skin on them in the room with me."

It is easy for me as a man to operate in the natural...to believe in what I see. I learned that *"doing what it took"* meant having a strong belief in God and the supernatural. I had to believe *more* in those things I could not see. I needed to believe...and act on the supernatural. I had to hang onto my faith until my miracle came. I had to change my thinking and believing. I had to change my personal walk with God and my personal relationship with Jesus. I began to believe that my heavenly Father was right there in the room with me...and in my mind He had skin on Him.

I found out that my closest friend in the world was my Heavenly Father. I now know I can pull up a chair next to Him and talk with Him and that He would listen. I personally met my Heavenly Father and became so close to Him that it seems as if He does have skin on Him when I look for Him in the room. In the Bible it says, "God is more than enough." I know that is true...he helped me *"do what it took"* to meet the challenges that faced our family.

CHAPTER TWELVE

TODAY'S MAN

"What should we do about the Women's Movement?"

Before the women's movement we knew exactly where we fit into the scheme of things. Men had their place and that was fine with us. But that's not true anymore. Traditional roles have changed. It is easy for us to feel off balance. We're not sure exactly how we should think and act about these changes.

More and more women are making contributions in medicine, science, entrepenuership, ministry, business leadership. They are virtually in every field...even in construction wearing a hard hat. Many women now make more money than their husbands or men they date. These are facts that most of us don't talk about but they are causing us to ask ourselves a lot of questions because we're not sure how to take it all. We have a lot of questions.

Should I open doors for women?

The world says it's up to you. God tells you to honor women. It is an action that tells everyone around you that you are considerate and respectful of women...and people in general. Not a bad message to send.

How should I feel when my wife makes more money than I do?

You should not feel threatened. Some jobs pay

more than others. It's as simple as that. Be proud of her. Her added income is a benefit. The amount of money each of you make should never be a source of competition between the two of you. Learn to value each other as individuals...not as money makers.

Does this mean I'm less of a man?

Remember, it is the world that says that your stature as a man is determined by the amount of money you make...not God. Money and success are things the world values. God values the way you treat and care for you wife. He values the way you train your children in spiritual things. When you take your place as a man of God and honor your family...*they* will honor you.

Do I have as much say in matters now that I don't have full responsibility for supporting my family?

Of course, money should not be the determining factor here. When you establish a Christian home where you both love and honor God and each other your worth is not dependent on the amount of money you make. If, however, you are domineering you can create *negative issues in your family.*

Being head of the family gives you authority but you should never operate with a controlling spirit. God should be in control of your life AND every member of your family should be controlled by God—not by you.

What if my wife has more knowledge than I do?

You live in America. There are libraries in abundance. You can have as much knowledge as you want. Knowledge and money should not become an issue if you value each other and have a strong Christain foundation in your family. You are full of whatever you have put spent your time to learn. Knowledge does not just fall on you. It takes discipline, time, and effort on your part to learn and fill yourself up with valuable knowledge and information.

My wife says she wants her own checking account and wants to establish her own credit. Is that OK?

We may think these actions are unnecessary but there are some things we should think about. If something were to happen to you, your wife could be without credit when she needed it the most. In a small midwestern town, a successful businessman died and had not made credit provisions for his wife. The woman was unable to get a credit card even though she was financially sound and her family had been pillars of the community for years.

I'm sure that you can think of other questions. If you have questions write to me...I'll be glad to give you my thoughts.

Have you ever stopped to ask yourself, *"What's good about this?"* Well, the fact is that there are some good things about the times in which we live. There have been some changes made in the home that can bring a family closer together. One of them is the fact that, today, couples are working together as a team to run the home and rear the children. The father has much more interaction with the children. In Christian homes women know the man is to be the spiritual head of the home. His position in the family is not destroyed, in fact, it is enhanced by his stronger involvement with his family.

Couples see their children as the responsibility of both mother and father...not just the responsibility of the mother. *Fathers are enjoying closer relationships with their children because of shared roles*. In the past, fathers were often distant, unavailable and always at work. Children didn't know how to relate to their fathers because they didn't know them.

There is something else taking place that is good...women have their own identity as well as having the identity of being a wife and mother. They feel good about their own personal worth and the goals they have set for their own lives. Therapists agree that "in order for a person to be emotionally healthy, they must experience a sense of personhood." It's not just something for today. Read Proverbs 31 and you will find a woman who was very much involved in her family, and a very successful business. This is not some long gone woman but I believe this is the "ideal woman" that God has already put within every female. I believe that she can grow into every aspect of the Proverbs 31 woman if she is nurtured properly by her husband.

There is an excellent Christian book called *Boundaries by Cloud and Townsend*. In the chapter entitled *Boundaries and your Spouse* they describe some of the boundary problems couples face. "When the two become one on their wedding day, spouses do not lose their individual identities. Each participates in the relationship, and each has his or her own life. Where boundaries can get confusing is in the elements of personhood-the elements of the soul that each person possesses and can choose to share with someone else. The problem arises when one trespasses on the other's personhood, when one crosses a line and tries to control the feelings, attitudes, behaviors, choices, and values of the other. They are things only each individual can control. There's that word again..."control." To try to control these things is to violate someone's boundaries, and ultimately, it will fail. *Successful relationships are based on freedom, not control.*

"One of the most important elements that promotes intimacy between two people is the ability of each to take responsibility for his or her own feelings." *When something is important to one of you and not the other, the person that feels its importance should creatively take the responsibility of making sure whatever it is gets done. Not dealing with hurt or anger can kill a relationship.*

Townsend and Cloud further say, *"Problems arise when we make someone else responsible for our needs and wants, and when we blame them for our disappointments.* Psalm 37:4 says, "Delight yourself." Just stop there and notice the understood subject. "you, delight yourself." No one else can do that for you, not even God. He won't delight you—you must do that and choose that for yourself. You delight in the Lord, *not* God will delight you. Every one must make up his own mind as to how much he should give. Don't force anyone to give more than he really wants to...Being aware of when we are giving past the love point to the resentment point. Any time you spend doing things for her is a gift from you; if you do not want to give it, you don't have to. Stop blaming your partner for everything.

"Passive boundaries, such as withdrawal, triangulation, pouting, affairs, and passive-aggressive behavior, are extremely destructive to a relationship. Passive ways of showing people that they do not have control over you never lead to intimacy. *They never educate the other on who you really are: they only estrange.*

"A hurt heart takes time to heal. You cannot rush back into a position of trust with too much unresolved hurt. That hurt needs to be exposed and communicated. If you are hurting, you need to own your hurt. Bring it into the light."

"Each spouse needs time apart from the relationship. Not just for limit setting, but for self nourishment. Many couples have trouble with this aspect of marriage. They feel abandoned when their spouse wants time apart. In reality, spouses need time apart, which makes them realize the need to be back together. Spouses in healthy relationships cherish each other's space and are champions of each other's causes."

"But that doesn't sound very submissive. First, both husbands and wives are supposed to practice submission, not just wives. "Submit to one another out of reverence for Christ" (Ephesians 5:21). Submission is always the free choice of one party to another. Wives choose to submit to their husbands, and husbands choose to submit to their wives."

"Whenever submission issues are raised, the first question that needs to be asked is, What is the nature of the marital relationship? Does the husband love his wife as Christ did the Church? Does she have free choice, or is she a slave "under the law"? Many marital problems arise when a husband tries to keep his wife "under the law," and she feels all the emotions the Bible promises the law will bring: wrath, guilt, insecurity, and alienation (Romans 4:15, James 2:10; Galatians 5:4) When the husband has to use threats instead of love to control the wife then something is very wrong.

"Often the husband is trying to get his wife to do something that is either hurtful or takes away her will. Both of these actions are sins against himself. 'Husbands ought to love their wives as their own bodies. He who loves his wife loves himself. After all, no one ever hated his own body, but he feeds and cares for it, just as Christ does the church' (Ephesians 5:28). Christ never takes away our will or asks us to do something hurtful. He never pushes us past our limits. He never uses us as objects. Christ "gave himself up" for us. He takes care of us as he would his own body.

"We have never seen a "submission problem" that did not have a controlling husband at its root. When the wife begins to set clear boundaries, the lack of Christ likeness in a controlling husband becomes evident because the wife is no longer enabling his immature behavior. She is confronting the truth and setting biblical limits on hurtful behavior. Often, when the wife begins to set boundaries, the husband begins to grow up.

"Learn to love in freedom and responsibility. Remember the goal of boundaries: *love comes out of freedom*. When you are in control of yourself, you can give and sacrifice for loved ones in a helpful way instead of giving in to destructive behavior and self-centeredness. This kind of freedom allows one to give in a way that leads to fruit. Remember, "No greater love has anyone than to lay down his life for his friends." This is to live up to the law of Christ, to serve one another. But this must be done out of freedom, not boundaryless compliance."

So be proud of your wife's accomplishments. It is a reflection on you. You and your wife are a team. You were able to attract this special woman into your life. Champion her victories and be there for her failures...she will love you completely for your support.

Today, some of the women, who thought they

wanted a career, are returning home. This is because women are realizing that they now have a career *and* the full responsibilities of the home. They are suffering from the "superwoman" role. They are realizing how good they had it without so many responsibilities. This is particularly true when there are children in the home.

However, there are still many women who prefer to keep working. They are finding fulfillment and a sense of accomplishment in their work. They are a woman and a wife as well as an individual who wants to achieve. We are husbands and fathers but we don't want to limit ourselves to these roles. We want to be individuals...and so do our wives.

We need to see our wives as individuals...and not just as our wives. It will change the whole atmosphere of your home when you respect your wife's person-hood. Learn to take pride in each others achieve-ments...and shoulder each other's failures.

There have been great advances in technology that allow women much more free time. Women are no longer totally occupied with running the home. They...like men, do not have to slave over their work. A woman can pursue a career—especially when the chil-dren are school age—and raise a family as well.

Change is difficult to deal with at first...because it is unfamiliar to us. We naturally want our families to operate as they have in the past. There are many things to be happy about. When a woman feels like a person who has accomplishments, she is happier about herself. When Mama's happy...we're happy!

CHAPTER THIRTEEN

THE IMPORTANCE OF MARRYING A CHRISTIAN WOMAN

There are many books written about marriage. When we read these books it tells us how important it is to have similar backgrounds, similar goals. They also tell us it is important that we "like" each other as well as "love" each other. The books talk about character strengths, too. But the fact is that men don't often select women for these reasons.

What is the one thing that we men look for above all else? Let's be honest. The most important thing to us is that our wife-to-be is attractive, right? In fact, we seem willing to overlook it if the woman has no character or faith. The important thing to us is, "Is she good looking?" It sounds pretty ridiculous, doesn't it? But it is the truth.

Now, you might be saying, "Well, I'm sure not interested in marrying an ugly woman." (I think they've even written Country Western songs about this!) Relax. I do not want you to marry someone that is not right for you. Nevertheless, let's discuss what is beautiful and what is ugly.

There is a saying, "All that glitters is not gold." What are you getting when you marry a woman *just* because she is beautiful? Many times women who are very attractive, and who have never experienced hardships in their lives, are very shallow. It has not been necessary for them to develop much character because their beauty has always been more than enough to meet the needs they have in their lives. This is because our society values appearance above all else, especially our male society.

When I first met Cheryl I looked at her inner beauty. It wasn't until we had been married five years, that I saw how physically beautiful she is. It all depends what you're focusing on.

Many of these beautiful women have decided to use their beauty to attract a wealthy husband. They will only date men who can take care of them financially and give them things. The men often understand what the women are doing...but they feel it is a good trade. Their money for her beauty.

This kind of superficial trade-off will never make you happy. Beauty is nice to see but in a marriage it takes *different qualities* to make you happy. In marriage both parties need to be givers to make it work. Selfishness can kill a marriage. You should always be looking out for each other's needs. You do things that will make each other happy...many of these things require hard work and dedication. They take care and consideration. Making sure the home is clean and attractive. She will raise your children in the care and admonition of the Lord. She will take part in PTA. She will entertain your friends and clients.

But above all else she needs to love you. She needs to be your biggest fan. She needs to encourage you. Ask yourself some questions. Does she build you up and make you feel as if you are capable of conquering

THE IMPORTANCE OF MARRYING A CHRISTIAN WOMAN

almost anything? Does she always take your side of situations...even when she finds it necessary to discuss areas that you may have overlooked? Or does she make you feel worse when things aren't going well? Some women are right there when there is money in the bank but when things are bad they distance themselves from you.

Ask yourself this. How would your wife-to-be communicate her anger? Does she talk to you gently about any faults you might have or does she ridicule and criticize you? Would she run you down to your children? When things are tense, does she cop an attitude? Or does she communicate, without criticizing, how she is feeling? Does your wife respect your parents? Would she be willing to share the grandchildren with your parents? Is anger her first reaction? Does "what about me" come out of her mouth?

When you first meet a woman there is a lot of surface appreciation between the two of you. When you get married you must live with many of the realities of life. Many a man has married a beautiful woman with no faith or character and grown to hate her. *When a beautiful woman is selfish her looks fade, you don't see her beauty, all you see is her weak character.*

True beauty comes from inside. I'm sure you know people that appeared homely when you first met them but after you got to know them you found they were truly beautiful. You couldn't wait to be around them. They are always so helpful, giving and loving. They don't appear to have a lot of problems. They are happy. They don't have a lot of baggage that comes with them. This kind of beauty wears well. You can be around this kind of person day in and day out. Your love grows for them because of their inner qualities. This is the kind of woman that makes a good wife.

Again, I'm not saying that you shouldn't marry a beautiful woman. What I am saying is that you need to focus on your wife-to-be's internal qualities. External beauty is great to behold but it is not enough to make you happy in a marriage.

If you want to be happy in a marriage, it is important that you marry a godly woman. As Cheryl says, "A Proverbs 31 woman!" Why is this important? The Bible says, *"Be not unequally yoked."* Why? Because when you have to deal with the hard issues of life you need someone with faith, love and courage.

There are many times that she will have to decide to do things just because they are honorable and right not because someone is making her live that way. A woman who truly loves God has a greater chance of making the right choices.

When the chips are down, a godly woman is much more likely to hang in there. Many women leave their husbands when there are financial problems or sickness. A godly woman responds to higher values. She trusts God that He will make a way where there is no way. Every action she takes is from the perspective of a Christian. She has Christian values.

Then there is the matter of finding peace and comfort in daily life. A woman who does not know Christ is often full of apprehensions. Her goals are to have more "things" and success. There is an underlying emptiness that she experiences...she does not have a God who will help her work on her problems or character flaws.

She is very likely to feel she "has rights" and that it does not matter what others around her need. The most important thing to her may be a career or success. She is inflexible many times...taking what she needs at the expense of others.

Now, don't get me wrong. Christian women are not perfect but when a woman loves the Lord she is much more likely to love you, too. When a woman or man has already learned to submit to the Lord they will be much more likely to submit to each other.

I know from personal experience that there are many beautiful Christian women! I'm married to a beautiful Christian woman. But the most important thing to me is the love my wife has for the Lord. Her faith directly impacts my life and the lives of my children. When Cheryl has a problem she talks to the Lord about it. She looks it up in the Bible. I don't just love my wife, "I'm in love with her." I love the way she is training our children to serve the Lord. She helps them learn Bible verses. She teaches our children that Jesus is important in our everyday lives. Once when Roman was sick he yelled at Cheryl from down the hall, "Mama, pray! Mama pray!" It was very natural for him to look to the Lord. I am impacting generations to come because I chose to marry a godly woman.

When a Christian woman experiences challenges in her life, she doesn't fall apart. The Lord helps her sort the problems out. She grows from the experiences. If there is no God involved in a woman's life she will go to a family member, friend or mentor for help. If these people are not Christians they can guide her and you toward problems.

I think it's important to realize that many women will tell you that they are Christians. Sometimes they will tell you what you want to hear. Ask them questions. Were your parents Christians? Did they take you to church? How often did you go to church? When did you receive your salvation? Do you read your Bible? How often do you read your Bible? Is she *hungry* for the things of the Lord? Or is she mildly interested? Is she a social Christian? Let her know that it is important to you that she love the Lord. This may seem like an interrogation but it's better to know than not to know.

If you are a Christian who has been A.W.O.L....absent without the Lord...you may want to return to your faith in the future. When you marry a woman who does not truly love the Lord you can end up going to church by yourself. You may be the one seeing to it that your children go to Sunday School. Your faith is ridiculed by your wife. Think about these things...they could happen!

Sometimes we go into a marriage believing that the woman will gain more maturity in the future or come to love the Lord. Or we think we can change her. Yes, this does happen sometimes. Unfortunately, the odds are not in your favor. The divorce courts are full of people who were unwilling to change. Divorce has risen over 200% since 1960. The fact is that the things that got on your nerves about your mate before you get married are magnified after you get married.

One of the problems that couples face is the idea of romantic love. They rush into a marriage because it feels good. They don't have any idea who the other person is in normal life. This is a good argument to take your time getting to know your mate before you marry her. As time passes, you will get to know whether you "like" the her. If you love her but do not like her...STOP...don't go any further with your relationship. When the emotional highs fade you will be living with a person you don't like or respect. This can be like living in a nightmare!

Many men *"live unconsciously."* They don't really think about these things. These men just "fall" in love. They feel so proud to have a beautiful woman on their arm that *they don't anticipate the problems up ahead.* They make decisions based on their emotions. Emotions help you appreciate a beautiful sunset but they aren't effective in making life-long decisions like who you should marry.

If you are interested in marrying a new Christian take the time to get to know her. Spend time together praying and reading your Bible. You will learn a lot about her faith level. If she is really hungry to learn about things of the Lord you can grow together. Her "hunger level" is very important.

One of the best ways to recognize faith is to have it yourself. Make some personal goals in your faith walk. Find a good church and go there regularly. Plan times to read your Bible...even if it's a few verses a day. Pray...talk to the Father like He is right there in the room with you...because He is! When you are in right standing with the Lord it will help you attract a godly woman in your life.

A Christian woman wants a man who loves the Lord. She has much to offer and she wants to invest it in the right place. She knows that it is important for her to marry a godly man. She knows her life and the lives of her children depend on it. She also knows that true happiness comes when you are "equally" yoked.

It is well worth it to *set a goal of marrying a godly woman.* It may be a little extra trouble to ask more in-depth questions of the woman you want to marry but it will pay off big in your future. The woman you marry will definitely impact your life, your children's lives and the lives of all your descendants. When faith passes from generation to generation it brings hope, happiness and a great way to live!

The opposite of passing a strong faith from generation to generation is passing dysfunction and unhappiness from generation to generation. If there has been dysfunction—codependency, alcoholism, drugs—in your family determine that it will stop with your generation. The devil will not have any place in your life or the lives of your family!

In Ephesians 4:27, it says, *"Don't give place to the devil."* When we allow things that are ungodly into our lives, we are standing in the path of destruction. If a tornado headed in your direction, you would get out of the path...because you know it could kill you. When you play with the things of the devil—bad movies, no Christian friends, alcohol, drugs, selfishness, greed, envy, an ungodly wife—you are standing in the path of destruction and you will experience pain from it. Remember, all the devil needs is a little foothold and he will come into your life full blown!

In the Old Testament God warned the Israelites that they were to stay away from idolatry. He told them not to become friends with idolaters. At that time, idolatry was graven images and false gods. God knew that marrying idol worshippers could cause them to leave their faith.

Your faith is the only thing that will bring you true happiness. We need to return to Christian values to discover true contentment and happiness. Many people today are experiencing depression, ill health, anxiety, dissatisfaction and a host of the devil's other ills, because they are not seeking God. Today, there is an onslaught of the devil like never before...it is not an optional decision...we must get close to the Lord.

When we make the decision that Joshua made, *"As for me and my house, we will serve the Lord,"* (Joshua 24:15) we bring the light of faith, hope and love into our families.

God wants to give us so much more than the world will give us.

The devil counterfeits the things of God...badly. The world and statistics say, "You can be married but it probably won't bring you happiness." God says that *"I came to give you life more abundantly."* When we establish a marriage by God's plan, we will experience a depth of love for our wife and children that the world will never know!

CHAPTER FOURTEEN

"FIND YOURSELF A CHRISTIAN BUDDY"

Today, there are many men who find themselves in the situation of having no Christian friends. They go to church but don't get involved in Sunday school or other small groups where they can meet other Christian men.

Maybe they are a new Christian. All of their old friends are not Christians. They don't have anyone they can talk to about the things of the Lord. The only way they sustain their faith is by going to a church service one hour a week and maybe reading Bible verses. If the time you spent at church was food...you would be a starving man!

When you find God it is one of the most important things you will ever do! You will have a better quality of life. You have a Source to go to who will never leave you or forsake you. You have countless promises from the Bible to help you every day of your life. You have a faith that you can pass on to your descendants. You receive spiritual *and* emotional healing.. The list goes on and on. It is great that you have made this decision.

What do you do now? It is important for you to get into a church that teaches the Word. Some churches give so few scriptures in their services that you could starve to death during the week. One hour a week focused on one or two scriptures is not enough to nourish your faith. So find a church that believes in strong teaching.

Word level is important in many ways. *"Faith comes by hearing and hearing by the Word of God."* (Romans 10:17) It is almost impossible to have faith if you don't know or understand what the Bible says. When you go to a church with a high Word level, it also protects you from ministers that preach the Gospel according to themselves. They tell wonderful stories but they do not give you the strong meat of the Word.

In past years, the church was the center of the community. You knew everyone in your church. You went to church and Sunday school together. You attended church socials and picnics. Today, it is very easy to attend a church where there are hundreds of people in several services. It is possible to walk into one of these churches, hear a great sermon and never speak to a soul you know.

If you are attending a church like this...that's OK. What you need to do is get involved in the small groups of your church. Many times you can attend home groups. Most of the time these churches have a wide assortment of groups, in which you can become involved. Make a goal to get involved. It is worth the effort.

Christian friends are important. When you don't have a Christian buddy you can talk to...it can get very lonely and discouraging. The guys you knew before are interested in different things. The things they want to do hold no interest for you now.

As a Christian you aren't interested in the things that you once were. Your old friends still want to do things that you did "in the good ole days." When you show no interest it creates a gap. *"Old things are passed away."* (II Corinthians 5:7) You're not the same person that you used to be. In fact, there may be such a difference in you now that you find it hard to imagine that you were "that same person." You don't want to hurt your old friend's feelings but you no longer have the same interests.

Christians should present salvation to the lost. That is what your former friends are...lost. They have not received their salvation. The Bible says that they will not go to heaven unless they turn their lives over to Christ. This is one decision that is black and white. You can't ride the fence on your salvation.

You may spend time talking to your friends about going to church or Bible study. They're not interested. They are living in the flesh and Satan's world and that's fine with them. Unfortunately, they don't know what they are doing. The devil has blinded them.

It is always important to try to witness to your friends but if they flatly do not want anything to do with God...you have a decision to make. Do you still want to hang out with your old buddies? After all, you guys have gone through a lot together. Ask yourself a few questions.

Do you feel good being around them anymore? Does it bother you that while you are together you don't feel comfortable talking about things of the Lord? (You've tried to witness to them and they don't want any part of it.) Does it bother you that they swear nonstop? Or even some? Do you like to go to bars or worldly events with them? You can talk to them about fishing, golf or other sports you both enjoy but you feel different from them now. In fact, sometimes you even feel yourself being drawn back into your old lifestyle. You hate it when that happens.

When you have a *Christian buddy*, that wants to learn more about God and try to become a better person, the two of you can support each other. You can help each other become better husbands, fathers, and friends.

You can go to men's prayer breakfasts or help at the church. Your buddy can go with you to Promise Keepers or Full Gospel Businessmen. The two of you can discuss about your problems together. When you watch God move in the lives of others it will strengthen your faith.

You will find that you feel uplifted and strengthened being around other Christians. We should always try to talk to the lost but when they refuse, we have to make a decision whether we want to "hang out" together. Jesus told the early apostles that they should preach the gospel in a town but if the people wouldn't listen, *they should shake the dust off their feet and move on.* Mark 6:11

Pray for your friends and tell them about the things of the Lord whenever possible but trying to be buddies like you used to be, can be dangerous.

Your goal now that you've accepted Christ should be to grow as a Christian and then tell others about the Lord. When you stunt your growth, by being around the lost all the time, it can take years to become a mature Christian.

God loves you and wants the best for you. He wants you to be strong in Him and ready to do His work!

— CHAPTER FIFTEEN —

OUR DIFFERENCES HELP US FUNCTION TOGETHER

In closing, I just want you to know and understand that God "designed" men and women to be different from each other. You're probably saying to yourself, "Well, of course we're different. That's obvious." That's the problem. We've focused on our external differences for a long time. We haven't understood the vital ways we "function" differently from each other. I believe that when we truly get in touch with how vital, beautiful, and useful our differences are, we will "celebrate" our differences. We will naturally move and function within these patterns God has instilled in us and consider them to be our strength...not our weakness. God instilled a strong desire in men to "fix things." He created women to be "menders."

What does that mean exactly? Visualize this. When you broke something as a child...who did you run to, to fix it? Your dad, right? It was natural for you to go to him. It didn't even matter to you that he might not be real mechanically adept. He was your dad and he was for fixing things. After the age of ten, I had no father so I either fixed my bike myself or asked a neighbor for help when something was broken.

As a child, I instinctively knew that when something

was broken...a man was supposed to fix it. Not only would he fix it, he would do it right then. NOW. Immediately! There was no fooling around. I noticed men weren't really interested in repairing, which takes a longer time, they wanted it fixed today!

The times I asked men for help I could see that it didn't really matter that they didn't have all the parts or tools to perform the task. They would just "rig something up" so they wouldn't have to disappoint the child or person asking for help. It was unthinkable for them to say, "I can't. Or, "Come back later when I have time to repair this." There's just something in his makeup that makes it hard for him to get those words out of his mouth!

Have you ever noticed how hard it is for a man to ask for directions? Men will drive miles before asking for directions. When they do stop to ask for directions they will have their wife ask the gas station attendant...all the while complaining about how bad the directions were in the first place. He may even blame his poor wife for writing down the wrong directions in the first place. You can be sure it wasn't the man who wrote the directions down wrong or the man who followed them incorrectly. Get the picture.

The fact is that not everything can be fixed on the spot...immediately. And God knew that. So He made provision for this by placing those responsibilities elsewhere. There are just some things that take time...things that need to be mended, repaired, and responded to over time.

That's where women come into the picture. Women are, by nature, menders. They mend things that are broken. Again, visualize yourself when you were a child. When you scraped your knee or tore your pants on a nail, there was no question in your mind who you would run to for help. When someone was hurt, you ran to mama...or the female figure in your neighborhood. You felt secure that you could count on her to comfort you, put your mind at ease...and explain the situation to you. Mama did these things so naturally, didn't she? It was just as natural for her to "mend" as it was for your dad to "fix things."

As a child, you could "sense" who was supposed to do what...even if the adults performing the functions weren't always aware of the natural functions they were performing. It didn't matter to you that your dad sometimes rushed to fix the problem and ended up with a badly repaired toy or appliance.

You always took it for granted that your mother would comfort, smooth over, soothe and take the time to heal any situation. That's because women are menders. In sewing, the word mend means not just sewing a stitch in a torn pant leg but taking the time to line up the two sides of the torn fabric and mend them together so you can't even see where the tear was. The area is restored to its original condition.

A man, on the other hand, wants everyone in the neighborhood to know he fixed it and how quickly he did it. He also wants to make sure everyone know that he didn't have the knowledge to do it but was able to do the job because of his superior intelligence. He expects everyone to run over and pat him on the back for his victory over the situation. He accepts the applause for performing the feat without knowledge of how to do it.

Now if you told him, before hand, that he should-n't try to fix something without knowing how to do it, he would tell you, you don't know what you're talking about. When a man is able to fix something—without knowing exactly how to do the task before he starts—it is a great victory to him. He overcame the odds!

It is important for us as men to remember that we can't fix everything! Sometimes you really need to listen to your wife...you'll be glad you did. I know. I will never try to fix a VCR again. The embarrassment of having to explain that I need both a TV and a VCR at the same time to the man at the TV store is just too much explaining. Your children will blow your cover any way, they will tell him the truth then and there. "Mommie tried to tell him!"

Men and women also react differently under stress. Men become assertive and women become emotional. Let me give you an example. When Cheryl's father died I wanted to know all the facts about the situation. I wanted to know where the funeral was to be held, when it was to be held, and what my responsibilities were before and at the funeral.

Cheryl's reaction was more in the emotional, sensitive realm. Her immediate question was "How is mama? How did he die? Where was he when he died? She began to cry because she is emotional by nature. She was comforted to know that he was not suffering anymore. She was glad he was in heaven. She did not cry for her sense of loss as much as the emotional nerve within her.

My reaction, and way of coping, was completely different from Cheryl's. I immediately proceeded to "get something done", and "take the bull by the horns." I had to attack the problem and resolve the problem for the good of all.

Here's another illustration that might be easier for

you to understand. When Lil Harry was five years old, we opened a clothing store in Tulsa. Before we opened the store it was necessary to set up the clothes racks and display tables. Cheryl was setting up the clothes racks and putting out the merchandise. I was in the back room with Lil Harry assembling equipment in the office. We were enjoying the prospect of our new project when all of a sudden I caught a glimpse of Lil Harry climbing up the front of a 200 pound metal filing cabinet. In a moment, the filing cabinet fell on top of him and pinned his head beneath its' weight. Lil Harry lay motionless in a pool of blood. I immediately pulled the cabinet off of him and yelled to Cheryl to call the doctor. I told her not to come into the back room until I asked her. Meanwhile, I took Lil Harry into the bathroom and washed the blood off of his face and hands so I could check the severity of the lacerations. I saw that his face was cut on the lip and cheekbone but nowhere else. His little barrel chest took the impact of the falling cabinet and then pitched it over on his head pinning his face to the floor causing gashes in his face.

After Cheryl called the doctor, she asked, "How bad is it? Can I come in and see?" I told her, "It's not bad and yes, you can come in now." You're probably wondering why I didn't encourage her to come into the room right away. I had a good reason. I didn't want her to see all the blood, become emotional and scare Lil Harry. I tried to play down the whole situation. It was my way of being assertive in the crisis...fixing and handling the situation.

You might ask, "Why didn't Cheryl just burst into the room with her motherly instincts to aid her child?" The reason is she has learned to trust my judgment. I was also very assertive in my attitude that everything was going to be all right. Cheryl rode in the van with us to the doctor's office. When we arrived Lil Harry was immediately taken to the examination room where they assured us that everything was going to be OK. At this point we moved into the mending stage...where the doctor was going to sedate Lil Harry and then stitch up the cuts in his face.

It was time for me to bow out. When we enter the mending stage, Cheryl takes over. She reassures and comforts Lil Harry telling him everything is going to be all right. She holds his hand and helps him deal with the accident on an emotional level.

I had dealt with the accident with an assertive attitude. "Get to the hurt child, clean him up, evaluate the situation, communicate the situation to Cheryl, get Lil Harry to the doctor." Now my job was done. I took one look at the needle used to sedate Lil Harry and out the door I went. I had used every endorphin in my body...there were no more left. It was Cheryl's job now. The next time I saw Lil Harry he had stitches in his face and a bandage over his eye. We left for the house where Mommie could nurse him back to health.

When we as men understand and value our wife's emotional nature we will function much better in our families. If a woman realizes that the man in her life is assertive by nature and that his "take over mentality" is not meant to put her down, they will have a much happier, fulfilled life and have a much stronger male/female relationship.

Assertiveness or aggressiveness can be positive...but it can also be negative. When a man does not have God in his life and experiences stress he can become physically aggressive. This is unacceptable, yet it happens. This may be a part of the male that was meant to protect his home and family but it must be kept in check.

Women are often aware that men can become physically aggressive when they are under stress and help their husbands avoid difficult circumstances. It is important to learn to walk away...to cool off. There is no situation that will become better through physical aggression. None. Ever. If you find this in your character you need to seek help or counseling.

It is always important to remember that God instilled these differences in us to help us function together. When both the husband and wife are aware of these differences and utilize them for an effective relationship...everyone is happy.

If you can relate to any one of the many things I have shared with you in this book and still haven't decided to make a change in your life, just do me one favor.

Take out a pencil and a piece of paper. Make two lists. Number them one to five. Five should be enough.

Example:

1.	1.
2.	2.
3.	3.
4.	4.
5.	5.

In the first list, write the things that are most important to you in your life. On the second list, write the things that you could do without if disaster struck (like Cheryl's illness). I'm sure that you can think of more than five things to put on your second list but just list the top five things that come to your mind.

I'll venture to say that when you study the lists of the most important things in your life and the items you could do without...they are completely opposites. When you look at the lists, the one you spend the most time and effort on is generally the list you can do without!

Here's my list. (A Sample)

1. Relationship with God.
2. Relationship with my wife.
3. Relationship with my children.
4. Relationship with my family.
5. Good health.

Could do without:

1. Compulsive work attitude.
2. Jewelry, home furnishings, car, etc. Monetary items.
3. Golf membership, outside family involvement's, social events.
4. Family vacations every year, new car every year.
5. Credit cards, savings account etc.

Life is made up of relationships and relationships are daily. They cannot be built in one day. Don't just think you can change on Sundays. You must make a change every day. Sunday is just a good day to start!

It's time to put

Relationships over Real Estate

Family over finances

Participating over providing

God over everything...

Friend, if you realize after reading my book that you have not made Jesus the Lord of your life, repeat this prayer after me.

"Jesus, I want you to come into my life and save me from my sins. I want You to be my personal Savior. I now know that I need your help to truly be a good husband and the head of my family. I need your wisdom, Lord. I can't do it alone. I need your guidance in carrying out this important role you have given me as head of my family. I love you, Lord."

Harry, I am enclosing my name and address and I ask that you pray for me and my family.

Name_____

Address_____

City_____State_____

Phone number_____

Salem Family Ministries

Order Form • P.O. Box 701287 • Tulsa, OK 74170

918-298-0770 Fax 918-298-2517

Title	Price	Qty	Total
Fight In The Heavenlies.............................$ 5.00		___	___
First in a series of children's action books			
For Men Only ....$ 7.00		___	___
A Royal Child ....$ 7.00		___	___
The Mommy Book ....$ 9.00		___	___
How God Can Find "Us" in an "I"			
"Me" Society (audio tape) ....$ 5.00		___	___
Family Matters (2 tape audio) ....$ 9.00		___	___
Be a Provider, Not Just A Participator (audio tape) ..$ 5.00		___	___
You Can Receive (video tape) $15.00		___	___
Testimony On Abuse (video tape) $15.00		___	___
Testimony On Depression (video tape) $15.00		___	___
Order Total		___	___

Shipping and Handling	Order Total	Shipping
	$0.00 – 10.00	$3.00
	10.01 – 25.00	$4.00
	25.00 – up	$5.00

Subtotal _____

Donation to Salem Family Ministries _____

Grand Total _____

Payment Method ☐ Cash ☐ Check ☐ Credit Card

Paying by Credit Card

☐ Visa ☐ MasterCard ☐ Discover

Credit Card # _____Expiration Date _____

Signature _____

Send Order To:

Name _____

Address _____

City _____State _____ZIP_____

Phone _____